Rekindling a Lost Passion

Recreating a Church Planting Movement

Russell Burrill

North American Division Evangelism Institute

HART RESEARCH CENTER
FALLBROOK, CALIFORNIA

Edited by Ken McFarland
Cover art direction and design by Ed Guthero
Illustration by Darrel Tank
Type set in 11.5/13 ITC Garamond Book

ISBN: 1-878046-53-5

Contents

About the Author

Russell Burrill, D. Min., is the Director of the North American Division Evangelism Institute in Berrien Springs, Michigan. He has served not only as a pastor and evangelist in many parts of the United States, but is also in great demand as a speaker and trainer.

In addition to presenting seminars on Bible prophecy to thousands across the United States and Canada and in overseas countries, Russell is at the forefront of today's renewed emphasis in the church on small-group fellowships, spiritual-gift-based church ministry, lay evangelism, and church planting.

As do his previous books, this volume explores revolutionary ideas on "reinventing" the church after New Testament and early Adventist patterns and practice.

Foreword

I am grateful for the passion that God has placed in Russell Burrill's heart for evangelism and church planting. The book you hold in your hands is the first Adventist book in modern times to provide a detailed strategy on "how to" plant a church. Russell not only provides the road map on how to plant a Seventh-day Adventist Church but on how to keep that new church focused on planting more churches. His strategy does not include planting churches just to redistribute the saints but specifically focuses on accomplishing the harvest!

Notice that church planting was not a new concept to the early church. Paul, the great missionary, was a church planter. His missionary journeys were really church-planting adventures. But planting Christian congregations started even before Paul. After the stoning of Stephen, Christians scattered to avoid the persecution in Jerusalem, but the end result was new congregations throughout Judea and Samaria. Acts 8:4 summarizes what happened: "And wherever they [the believers fleeing Jerusalem] were scattered, they told people the Good News" (NCV).

Church planting has again become an important initiative throughout North America. Our pioneers were church planters. Early Adventist pastors planted a church, trained lay leaders to keep the church going, then moved on to plant other new churches. Somewhere along the way we in North America lost the vision of church planting. We became content to keep the lights shining in existing churches, and we stopped lighting lights on new hills.

But recent evidence shows that we are turning around—from being a division that was losing churches to a division planting churches at a rate of ten every month! This is a tremendous change—a God-inspired and God-blessed change. It is a change that I personally longed for, prayed for, and challenged leaders, pastors and members to work for. It is a change that brought us back to our roots as a church-planting denomination. What helped initiate this change? Much of it has to do with a "Seeds" church-planting convention that the North American Division Evangelism Institute conducted at Andrews University in the summer of 1996 (now an annual event).

We chose to ask a church-planting expert from another denomination to explain church planting to us. We didn't have anyone ready to train the people who attended Seeds '96. In the future, the entire Seeds convention can be led by Adventists—Adventists who know church planting, who have done church planting, who have studied church planting, and who can explain it within the context of Adventism.

I am proud of those in North America who are taking the gospel to everyone in our territory. Guided by the Holy Spirit and demonstrating a living connection with Christ, they are reaching more and more people with Bible truths about a loving God and His last-day church. New congregations are springing up, fulfilling Jesus' words to His earliest disciples: "This is to my Father's glory, that you bear much fruit, showing yourselves to be my disciples" (John 15:8, NIV).

It is my prayer that in reading this book, a passion will be kindled in your heart for the mission God has given to each member of His church—to turn the twenty-first-century world upside down for Him.

Alfred C. McClure, President
North American Division, Seventh-day Adventist Church

1

A Passion for the Lost

I want you to meet two people. The first is "unchurched Sally." Sally is a typical forty year old. She is married a second time and has three children, two from her first marriage and one with her present husband. Her husband sells used cars, and Sally works as manager of one of the local banks. Caring for three kids, keeping up with the home, and holding down their jobs leave Sally and her husband exhausted by the weekend.

Neither Sally nor her husband attended church in their youth, but lately they have been searching for some stability and meaning in their lives. Having been exposed to some New Age philosophies, they have been experimenting with meditation. They long for a spiritual force in their lives, but nothing has satisfied their soul longings thus far. Since going to church has not been a part of their heritage, they have not even considered seeking meaning through the church. They are not negative to Christianity; in fact, they actually have positive feelings about the Christian faith. They have observed Christians who work with them, but see little difference in the lives of these coworkers, apart from the fact that they go to church each week. Sally and her husband desire something deeper than they see in the lives of their Christian friends; therefore they have ruled out the church as a source for spiritual life.

The second person is "churched Peter." Peter attends "Community Church" every week. He enjoys the weekly worship service and the community activities provided by the church. He is glad to be part of a church that is really trying to impact his community. He knows that the church teaches basic morality, and he is happy that his children can readily receive these moral teachings.

When asked about his beliefs, Peter tells us he feels that as long as he lives a good moral life, he and his family will go to heaven. When asked about Satan, Peter indicates that he believes Satan is just a name for evil but not an actual entity. When questioned about the Ten Commandments, Peter tells us that he feels they are good, but he can't recall more than two or three of them. One he does remember, however, is the one about God helping those who help themselves.[1] When asked if he obeys the Ten Commandments, Peter responds that it depends on the situation. Yet down deep, Peter feels that something is missing. He wishes he had more peace in his life, but then he puts the doubts out of his mind, contenting himself with the thought that at least he goes to church every week.

Who is God calling Seventh-day Adventists to reach: unchurched Sallys or churched Peters? The answer is, both. Our message has been commissioned by God to unshackle both the Sallys and the Peters of this world. What many have not realized is how drastically the religious climate of North America has changed over the last few years.

Secularism is dead. We now live in the post-secular age; it is not a Christian age, but a post-Christian age. People are spiritual, but they are not excited by Christianity's spirituality, as evinced by those who claim to be Christians. The secular people of the 80s and early 90s are now caught up in

New Age philosophies and eastern religious mysticism. They are not irreligious—just not interested in Christianity. George Barna declares that the reason Christianity is so unappealing to these people is that they have not seen that Christianity makes any difference in people's lives. They view Christians as different only in the fact that they go to church once a week; otherwise, they have the same problems as do non-Christians. There is no advantage, then, in becoming a Christian. Therefore, they look elsewhere to fulfill their spiritual longings.

Not only has the climate of the unchurched changed, but so has the status of the churched. Just because people attend the most visible event of the local church—the weekly worship service—they are not necessarily Christians. Barna indicates that they may be ignorant of the basics of the faith, as in the case of "churched Peter." Is everyone who attends church like "churched Peter"? Obviously not. Many are sincere and biblical Christians. However, Barna reports that only 10 percent of Americans can be considered what he calls "biblical Christians." That would mean that fully *90 percent* of Americans are not biblical Christians. Two hundred and forty-three million out of two hundred and seventy million Americans are not biblical Christians. What a harvest needing to be reaped in America! Only two or three other countries of the world have more nonbiblical Christians. America is one of the greatest mission fields on the planet, and the number of unreached people is growing.

Barna's research divided Americans into seven different religious groups:

1. Biblical Christianity. These are people who fully accept the authority of the Bible, place their total trust in Christ for salvation, are involved in evangelism, are active participants in the life of their church, are seeking continuously for a more intense spiritual development, and believe in moral absolutes. They are only 10 percent of the American population.

2. Conventional Christianity. These people place their total trust in Christ for salvation, are involved in the life of the church, and appreciate the Bible. However, they have made religion a private matter, rarely share their faith, and their lives are only vaguely influenced by their faith. To them morality is relative. They account for 25 percent of the U.S. population.

3. Cultural Christianity. This large group of people are basically universalists and trust in a works-based theology. They have nominal church involvement, attending only once or twice a year, or use the church for "hatching" and "dispatching" (baptism and burial). They are Christian in name and heritage only. To them morality is relative. They comprise about 28 percent of the population.

4. New Age Practitioners. To them, faith is a totally private matter. Truth is relative, not absolute. You can find truth in all religions. In fact, they have drawn their religious principles from a variety of faith traditions. They recognize no centralized religious authority. The deity they serve is intermingled with self, and they are more focused on religious consciousness than on religious practice. They comprise 19 percent of the American population.

5. Jewish. These people adhere to the traditional Jewish faith and comprise only 1 percent of the U.S. population.

6. Atheist/Agnostic. These individuals are oblivious to the faith realm, denying or doubting the existence of God. They are not seeking an experience with God and are the remnants of secularistic faith. They only comprise 9 percent of Americans.

7. Other. These are adherents of an amalgam of faith groups or to highly individualistic perspectives on spirituality. Among groups included here would be Islam, Mormonism, Buddhism, and Hinduism. These comprise another 8 percent of the population.[2]

How are Adventists doing in reaching these people groups? Recent research has indicated that Seventh-day Adventists are doing a better job of reaching the "unchurched Sallys" than almost any other denomination. The only Christian group doing better is the nondenominational grouping of churches. Yet Adventists do almost as well as they.[3] Adventists' evangelistic strength has been in reaching unchurched people rather than churched people. Regale's research actually indicated that Adventists do a below-average job in reaching churched people and convincing them to change denominations.[4]

This latest research actually indicates a major shift in the religious landscape of America. In no era of American history has there been such a lack of biblical Christianity. Fully 90 percent of Americans are unevangelized, even by non-Adventist standards. Yet in spite of the great lack of biblical Christianity in America, there is a deep spiritual longing. Seventy-four percent of American adults indicate that it would be very desirable to have a close relationship with God. Sixty-eight percent claim that they have felt that they were in the presence of God at some time in their lives.[5]

People today are not rejecting faith—they are craving faith. They earnestly desire an experience with God. They want to reach out and touch Him and know that He is real. This leaves them wide open for deceptions that emphasize feeling over the Word. We must offer them the real thing—the Word of God that leads to a dynamic experience with Jesus.

God has called the Seventh-day Adventist church into existence for such a time as this. We are called by God to go forth and claim this great harvest for God. This mission of the Adventist church becomes clear only as we discover the passion of God for lost people. That passion has been fully revealed in both the Old and New Testaments.

The Passion of God

The great passion of God for the lost is vividly seen in the fall of the human race. God's perfect creation sinned. Genesis 3:1-6 tells the sad story of the fall of our first parents.

However, in their fallen state Adam and Eve did not begin their search for God. In fact, the opposite occurred—they went into hiding from God. They covered themselves with fig leaves and hid in the bushes to escape Him. This is the natural state of the human race—hiding from the presence of God. Humanity does not naturally seek God; instead, they attempt to escape Him.

Into the darkness that humanity had created for itself came God. He took the first step to reconcile humanity. He did not wait for Adam and Eve to discover their need of Him—He came to them in their state of "hiddenness." God goes in search of humanity. As He entered the garden, He literally shouted out, "Adam, Eve, where are you?"[6]

Here is a picture of God we must never forget. He is a God who is searching, a God who is longing to restore broken relationships, a God who does not wait for us to return but comes seeking us, a God who initiates the seeking. The phrase "Where are you?" is in the background of everything else in Scripture. The rest of the Bible simply unfolds the story of God's unrelenting search for this humanity that is living in rebellion against Him.

Moses did not go down to Egypt to deliver his people. God first called Moses to be the deliverer. God put no requirements on Israel until He had delivered them purely by His grace.[7] He found them in sin and delivered them, not because of anything they did, but purely out of His great love for them.

The most dramatic Old Testament example of God's seeking the lost is the vivid drama of Daniel and Nebuchadnezzar. God's attempt to reach this heathen king is seen through the metallic image dream of chapter 2, the appearance of the Son of Man in the fiery furnace in chapter 3, and ultimately the vision and reality of Nebuchadnezzar's insanity which finally results in Nebuchadnezzar's finding God.

God's further seeking of the lost is revealed by His persistence in causing his prophet Jonah to take the first submarine ride. This occurred because God intensely longed to see the lost people of Nineveh come to faith in Him. As a result of Jonah's preaching, the whole city was brought to a knowledge of God. This illustrates that God can use even reluctant witnesses in His effort to reach the lost.

God's insatiable desire to save lost people is ultimately revealed in Jesus' first advent. Why did He come? To seek and to save the lost.[8] The Incarnation and Christ's death on the cross reveal the great, searching heart of God and His intense desire for lost people to be found and brought to faith.

The great passion of Jesus for the lost is seen in the many statements He made about them:

"I am not come to call the righteous, but sinners to repentance;" "They that are whole have no need of the physician, but they that are sick;" and the parables of the lost sheep, the lost coin, and the lost son.[9]

All of these reveal that God's ultimate purpose in sending Jesus was to find lost people and bring them to faith. Jesus constantly upset "churched" people because of His passion for getting close to lost people. He was known as a friend of publicans and sinners. Churched people were upset with Him because He was so enthusiastic about reaching the lost and the outcasts of society.

When lost people get found, it calls forth the ultimate expressions of joy. All heaven explodes in rapturous praise. The Bible story is all about the great God who finds lost people—the God who does not wait for lost people to come to Him but who constantly searches for them. Listen to the joy experienced when the lost get found:

> I say unto you, that likewise joy shall be in heaven over one sinner that repenteth, more than over ninety and nine just persons, which need no repentance.

> Likewise, I say unto you, there is joy in the pres-

ence of the angels of God over one sinner that repenteth.

And the seventy returned again with joy, saying, Lord, even the devils are subject unto us through thy name.

And there was great joy in that city.

And the disciples were filled with joy, and with the Holy Ghost.

. . . declaring the conversion of the Gentiles: and they caused great joy unto all the brethren.

For what is our hope, or joy, or crown of rejoicing? Are not even ye in the presence of our Lord Jesus Christ at his coming?

. . . who for the joy that was set before him endured the cross, despising the shame, and is set down on the right hand of the throne of God.[10]

No wonder all heaven explodes with joy whenever lost people come to God! This event excites all heaven—they can't help themselves! It is just part of their nature. They get excited and passionate about what God gets excited and passionate about—lost people coming to God! That is why we see joy in heaven and joy in the church on earth when lost people get found.

What does this reveal about God? That lost people matter to Him, and that finding them is the top priority of heaven. God cannot help Himself; He keeps seeking, no matter what people have done. No one can run so far away that God cannot find them. No matter where they go, God follows. He does not leave the lost in the pit of lostness, He comes seeking them.

Jesus' great sympathy for lost people moved Him to tears throughout His ministry. The cry of the multitudes of the lost moved Him to great compassion:

And when he saw the multitudes he was moved

with compassion on them, because they fainted and were scattered abroad, as sheep having no shepherd.

And Jesus went forth, and saw a great multitude, and was moved with compassion toward them.[11]

Every time Scripture declares that Jesus was moved with compassion, it is always at the sight of lost people. Yet it was not just the lost condition of people that moved the heart of Jesus but the fact that God's shepherds were not finding them. Christ was moved to tears by the needs of lost people and the failure of His people to feel His passion for them. His people were "playing church" while the lost were scattered and alone. What seemingly moves Jesus to the very depths of His being is the sight of lost people who want to be found, and the failure of God's people actually to reach out and fill the great void in the hearts of the lost. Nothing moves Jesus more than the unchurched Sallys and churched Peters of the world. Note His response in Matthew 9:37, 38:

The harvest truly is plenteous, but the labourers are few; Pray ye therefore the Lord of the harvest, that he will send forth labourers into his harvest.

The cry of the harvest Lord is that lost people be reaped. They are searching in forbidden fields and drinking from polluted streams. They desperately need the unvarnished, untarnished, unadulterated Word of the Living God.

The Mission of the Church

If it is inherent in the nature of God to seek for the lost, if this seeking is at the very core of who God is, then those of us who have been reconciled to God will partake of His seeking nature. Just as God cannot help but continually seek lost humanity, so those in whom the character of God is being reproduced will constantly be involved in seeking the lost. This will be the very heart of the mission of the church, because all of God's seeking must be done through humans.

Seeking lost people and reconciling them to God is not an option for Christians; it is at the very center of what it means to be a Christian. Not to be involved in God's seeking ultimately means not to be involved with God, because the passion of the seeking God is for lost people to be found. Having been reconciled to God, the seeking heart of God now burns deeply within my own heart. Like God, I cannot help myself; I have to be involved in finding the lost. When this happens, the thing that breaks the heart of God will break my heart. The sight of the lost will move me as it moves God.

Here we are not talking about nameless millions of people who do not know biblical Christianity. We are talking about Mary, Sue, John, Jeremy, Dave, and Elaine—people you know; people you see every day. They sit next to you at the office, you share garden produce over the back fence with them, you brush against them as you walk down the street every day. Look into their eyes as you walk the streets of your community. These are not nameless people to God.

Does the sight of these people move you to tears, as it moved Jesus? Does the cry of the harvest reach to your ears? These people, as sheep without shepherds, are lost, wandering, searching for they know not what. We have not yet done our job—there is a mighty harvest that God is calling us to reach.

Not only are people lost; they are also searching for meaning in life. The good news is that they want to be found. That's why many of them are seeking New Age philosophies. Why is "Touched by an Angel" one of the most popular TV shows at the end of the twentieth century? Why does NBC air prime time programs such as "Amazing Prophecies," featuring the prophecies of psychics and New Age philosophers such as Nostradamus? Why is the Star Wars trilogy still so popular? All of these reveal humanity's great longing for spiritual things.

People are seeking true prophecies, but they are drinking from polluted waters. They need Adventism's prophetic mes-

sage. This is not a time to discard our prophetic approach—
it is a time to proclaim the prophecies with renewed vigor.
Multitudes are ready to be reached, and if we do not share
with them the gospel of Christ, someone or something else
will fill the void. Hungry people will eat anything. The state
of North America today is such that there are lots of hungry
people eating forbidden fruit because we have failed to share
with them the precious fruit of the gospel of Jesus Christ.
These people are like Israel of old, crying out to God for
deliverance. That cry of slaves in ancient Egypt moved God
to send Moses to deliver them.[12] Those ancient Israelites were
not crying for Moses. They did not know what they were
crying for; they just wanted deliverance. So with the modern lost; they are crying to God, whom they do not know.
They don't know what they need; they only know they need
something.

God hears the cries of this multitude. He has declared that
the harvest is ripe and plenteous.[13] Do we hear the cry? Have
we seen this plenteous harvest that God has prepared? This
passion for the lost must grip us as it grips the heart of God.
It must grasp us with such force that nothing has higher priority in our churches than the salvation of the lost. That is
the priority of heaven, and any church with its priorities in
any other order is outside the will of God.

The church, then, is called to join God in His seeking ministry. Yet the church must not be engaged in seeking because
of its own need—the budget would benefit if more people
were in church, we would feel more comfortable if the pews
were filled, or because it would be nice to have a larger
church. All of these reasons are selfish, and God cannot bless
our seeking for selfish reasons. Sometimes Adventists seem
to want to seek so that the work can be finished and we can
go home. That, too, is selfish. We don't care about the lost;
we only care about our salvation. No wonder God has a hard
time with our selfishness!

Our seeking must be motivated by the love of God in our
hearts, because we, like God, cannot help ourselves. We so

long to see the lost come to Christ that we are willing to make any changes necessary in our individual lives and in our church to reach lost people and bring them to Christ. We seek because it is the character of God to seek, and the church is to be a reflection of God's character. We seek because God's passionate love for lost people is being reproduced in us, His children. Thus we, like Jesus, are moved to great compassion to reach out and find God's lost people.

The reason for the existence of the Seventh-day Adventist Church

God elected His ancient people, Israel, to be the seekers of the heathen for God. They were elected not because they were better than anyone else, but because God chose them to join in His seeking ministry. They were elected for the sake of the nations that did not know God. Israel, however, became self-satisfied and felt that they were better than everyone else, as if they had discovered God all by themselves rather than God revealing Himself to them. When Israel reached this point, they went into captivity and ultimately lost their exclusive right to be the carriers of God's mission to the world. While rejected as a nation, individually they were still chosen.

Likewise, God has raised up the Seventh-day Adventist Church and chosen it to be His remnant people in these closing days of earth's history. Why has God called this church to be the remnant? Because its members are more important to God than anyone else? No! The Seventh-day Adventist Church was called into being to proclaim the remnant message, so that the world might be brought to the saving knowledge of Christ and His truth for the closing hours of Planet Earth.

If Adventists cease to be intimately involved in God's seeking ministry, they, like Israel of old, stand to be rejected by God, not as individuals but as a church. Imagine McDonald's keeping open and subsidizing a franchise that had sold only one hamburger in the last ten years! Impossible! Of course,

McDonald's knows that it exists to sell hamburgers. If a franchise fails to sell enough, it loses the "privilege" of selling McDonald's hamburgers, and the franchise goes to a different owner. The Adventist church exists for the sake of making disciples for Jesus. If we fail to do so, then, as with an unproductive McDonald's, we will lose the right to the franchise and it will be given to another. Adventists do not believe in unconditional prophecy. If you doubt the verity of this illustration, reread Matthew 21:33-46.

If we fail to seek the lost, God will raise up others to find them, but we will lose the privilege of being involved in that seeking ministry. When a church ceases to be an evangelistic agency involved in the mission of the seeking God, that church ceases to be the true church, because mission is at the heart of the seeking God. Any church labeled "Seventh-day Adventist" that is not actively reaching and winning the harvest for God is not a true Seventh-day Adventist Church, no matter what the sign says. It is time to give the franchise to another!

What is the difference between a swamp and a stream? A swamp collects water, but a stream has an outlet. Any church that is not reaching out has become a swamp! Throughout the years, the church has sought to contain the seeking God for itself, but God's plan is that the church be the people of God for the sake of the nations, those who do not know God.

If the church exists for the purpose of reaching people for God, then the church building and property do not exist to serve the membership of the church but to aid that membership in being a part of the seeking heart of God. That is why the building, the worship services, and the outreach of the church must be "user friendly." All must be designed and utilized for the sake of the one who does not know Christ. For this reason, we need to ask what our worship services would mean to a visitor. This is not a call to lower standards, but for a deliberate strategy designed to reach the lost.

User friendly churches design their services to reach people where they are, rather than expecting the lost to come to where the "saints" are. That's why Jesus commissioned His church to "go" rather than simply to invite people to "come." The church is the one organization that does not exist to serve its present membership—it exists for the sake of those who do not know God.

The ultimate example of this incarnational approach to ministry was that of Jesus Himself. He did not sit on the ivory throne of the universe and ask us to come up to Him. He left the throne and was born in a stable, where the first smell that greeted his nostrils was the smell of manure. Why did He do it? Because He wanted to become one with us to reach us where we were. In this way Jesus demonstrated what He taught. In carrying out the Great Commission, His followers were to incarnate the gospel into every culture and every people group. Gentiles did not have to become Jews in order to become Christians. Christianity was made culturally appropriate to every group it reached. This is at the heart of Paul's poignant statement on incarnational ministry:

> For though I am free from all men, I have made myself a slave to all, that I might win the more. And to the Jews I became as a Jew, that I might win Jews; to those who are under the Law, as under the Law, though not being myself under the Law, that I might win those who are under the Law; to those who are without law, as without law, though not being without the law of God but under the law of Christ, that I might win those who are without law. To the weak I became weak, that I might win the weak; I have become all things to all men, that I may by all means save some. And I do all things for the sake of the gospel, that I may become a fellow partaker of it.[14]

Paul did not compromise one iota on principle, but he continually adapted his methodology to reach people where they were. Churches today that follow the incarnational approach to ministry will continually be changing their methodologies to reach the changing needs of people. Yet they will be inflexible when it comes to the basic message of Christ and Adventism. People must be reached where they are, but they must be reached with the real thing: untarnished Adventism. This is not a call to compromise our faith but a plea to use and discover new methods to reach new groups of people. Listen to what Ellen White said about innovation:

> The methods and means by which we reach certain ends are not always the same. [You] . . . must use reason and judgment. . . . Different methods of labor are to be employed to save different ones. Different methods of labor are really essential. New methods must be introduced.

> As field after field is entered, new methods and new plans will spring from new circumstances. New thoughts will come with the new workers who give themselves to the work. As they seek the Lord for help, He will communicate with them. They will receive plans devised by the Lord Himself.

> Church organization . . . is not to prescribe the exact way in which we should work. . . . There must be no fixed rules; our work is a progressive work, and there must be room left for methods to be improved upon.

> Some of the methods used in this work will be different from methods used in the past, but let no one, because of this, block the way by criticism. There is to be no unkind criticism, no pulling to pieces of another's work.[15]

One of the most difficult tasks for churches is to keep the balance between the world and the church. Throughout its history the church has continually leaned to one extreme or the other. Either it becomes a mighty fortress and shuts the world out, or it becomes so much like the world that little difference remains. God's church must avoid both extremes. It dare not become so isolated from the world that it no longer relates to the people of the world. Otherwise its members become so well adapted to the world of the church that they no longer know how to fish. At the same time, the church must not become a consumer church, where we seek to become so much like the world that the lost fail to see the church as a place that can change their lives.

The church calls people out of the world and brings them to Jesus, who redeems them. They are then returned to the world to reach and transform it. Satan would prefer the church to advocate the two extremes rather than the biblical view of transformed people impacting the world for Christ, yet such an impact by Christians is what the world so desperately needs in this degenerate age.

God's Harvest is Ready

The world today urgently needs Christians as transforming agents to move into the world and claim it for Christ. Matthew 9:38 declares that the harvest is ready to be gathered. We have not prepared the harvest, but Christ has, for He is Lord of the Harvest. "Therefore urge the owner of the harvest" (Lamsa translation), "the Lord to whom the harvest belongs" (Knox translation). We are merely God's instruments to reach out and claim this great harvest for Him. We don't have to go out and prepare this harvest—the message of Jesus is that the harvest is ripe. God has done His work. The harvest is prepared. All that are needed are laborers to go and reap it.

Since it is God's harvest and He has prepared it, we must give God all the glory for the harvest. It is not ours to claim. Yet God has a problem with this harvest. Although it is ready and prepared, God needs reapers, because He does not reap. That is our part. He sends us forth to garner. That's why the heart cry of Jesus is for more reapers in the harvest field. When we hear the cry of the lost as God hears it, then the cry of the saved will be that of Matthew 9:38: "Beseech the Lord of the harvest to send out workers into His harvest" (NASB).

The great need of the church today is for an increase in reapers. Faithful Christians need to beseech the Lord of the harvest to impress more people to go out into the harvest field and glean the harvest which God has prepared. As Christians pray, God will say "Go." Immediately following the call for prayer for more laborers, Jesus sent forth the twelve to preach the good news.[16] In Luke's rendering of the cry for more laborers, Jesus sent out the seventy. Clearly the prayer for reapers is a personal prayer that results in a person's going into the harvest field.

The immensity of the harvest and the challenge of the Great Commission to make disciples among all people groups calls for two kinds of reapers. First are individuals who will find their friends and acquaintances and introduce them to Jesus, and second are individuals whom God has called to go forth and plant new churches to reach God's harvest.

This is a book about church planting. It will give you the "nuts and bolts" about planting a church. But church planting is not just strategy and plans—it is reaping the harvest. New churches must not be established merely to redistribute the saints. New churches are demanded by the Lord of the harvest in order that the lost might be found. Existing churches simply cannot manage the harvest that God wants to send. New churches are required to reach new people groups, thereby extending the kingdom of God farther and farther.

All the methodology in the world will not help us plant successful churches until we feel the <u>urgency</u> which God feels for the salvation of lost. This thought needs to so possess us that we cannot sleep at night because of the many people who need to be found. When <u>God's passion for the lost grips us,</u> we will not be able to drive the streets of our great cities and observe the teeming masses of humanity without being moved to tears for their salvation.

Too Many Small Churches

"If we start many new churches, the result will be a lot of small churches, and we don't need more small churches," some say. The trend in the church growth movement, and even in some parts of Adventism at the close of the twentieth century, has been to attempt to create mega churches with attendance in the thousands. Many have felt that this is the ideal. The power, the prestige, and the feeling of success generated by such churches have allured some. Others have been more properly motivated to reap a large harvest for God.

However, the mega church movement has not been too successful among Adventists. We have created few such churches except in institutional settings. This has created frustration and unrest. In some cases there has been the feeling that if only we had the financial power at the local church level that other local churches have, we could do it, too. Are large churches the answer to reaching the harvest?

Recent research by Christian Schwarz, a German missiologist, revealed that large churches actually were the third most negative factor toward growth.[17] Successful mega churches, he discovered, were the exception, not the rule. That is the reason that everyone brags about them—they are an aberration, not a normal occurrence. Schwarz discovered that small churches were actually *1600 percent* more effective in reaching the harvest than mega churches.[18]

George Barna, a major trend watcher for the church, predicts that decentralization in the wider world will affect the church in the next century with a growing number of smaller churches, a redefinition of the pastoral roles, and greater integration of the laity into ministry.[19] In examining this trend, Barna suggests that the mid-size church may actually be squeezed out. It is not small enough for personal relationship and not big enough for the variety of options needed.[20] So the small church may be "in" as we enter the twenty-first century.

The result of fulfilling God's priority

In view of the Master's call for more reapers and the priority of reaping the great harvest the Lord has prepared, the church must respond. Existing churches should prioritize their time, talent, and treasure for reaping God's harvest and begin to think of unreached people groups in their territory for which a new church plant will be needed. Pastors need to be freed to evangelize and plant churches and cease to "hover over the churches."[21] Churches need to learn how to care for themselves and become less pastor-dependent.[22]

The vast army of laity in the Adventist church needs to be equipped to become reapers of God's harvest. The Adventist church must once again become a lay movement in which the laity are empowered to reach the lost, care for the church, plant new churches, and be involved in decision making at all levels of church administration. All areas of ministry must be fully restored to the laity—preaching, teaching, evangelism, church boards, committees, etc.

The church must cease to offer laity only a piece of the pie—they must be offered the *whole pie*. Lay people are not *part* of the church; they *are the church*. The word *laity* comes from the Greek "laos," meaning "people." Laity are thus the people of God, and that means all of us, clergy and laity together, with all separation removed. so that we once more become the totally unified people of God for the sake of the nations that do not know God.

Why issue such a clarion call for a lay- and mission-driven church? Because the hour is so late. Jesus is soon to come. The harvest is overripe. The reaping process is enormous. It is therefore time to put away our minor differences and concentrate on that which unites us rather than that which separates us. Then we shall be totally united in the passion of Christ for lost humanity.

Several years ago the *Adventist Review* published a heart-wrenching parable that illustrates so well what this chapter has sought to convey:[23]

The old man awoke and glanced at the clock. Shock registered on his aging face as he realized that he had slept too long. The tide would be coming in and his three youngest children were still out collecting shells on the island. He leaped through the door and ran toward the beach, stumbling over the jagged, cutting rocks.

"My children, my children!" he shouted. "Someone help my children!" He could see the little island and the rising water between it and the shore. He could faintly make out the outline of the three small bodies against the rugged rocks. "My children will drown. Oh, God, my babies will die. Someone help me!" The water was rising. Only a matter of time. Higher and higher.

A short distance down the beach he saw a group of picnickers. They would help. His legs nearly buckled as he ran. Nearing the group, he saw his older sons.

"Sit down, Father, and join our potluck. Here's a chair. We were just wishing that you could be here with us. We wanted to tell you how much we love you."

"You'd better rest a minute, Father. You shouldn't run like that at your age. What's the trouble?"

"The island—the little ones are out there. They're going to die!" Great sobs tore through his body.

"Now, Father, calm down! I'm sure it isn't that bad. Look, the rocks are above water." John clumsily patted the old gray head, then lifted his father's face to his. "Take it easy. We're here with you, and we love you very much."

"But you don't understand. The tide is rising. Oh, my babies! Please, oh, please, help me."

"There's no rush, Father. Don't let yourself get

so worked up. It's not good for your heart. We'd die if anything happened to you. Say, look. There are Joe and Dave and their new lifesaving boat. They're more able to help than we are."

The weary father turned away and shouted into the wind. Joe and Dave, other sons of his, heard and came in to shore.

"Save the children! The island will be covered soon!"

They seemed to understand and strong hands pulled the weeping man into the boat. Then the eager motor sprang to life and they headed out to sea. In the distance he could see three tiny figures clutching the highest rocks as the waves washed about their feet.

"Hurry, please hurry," he cried.

"Yes, Father, we understand. This is a lifesaving boat and it's really grand. We brought it over today just to show it to you. Look—padded seats, air-conditioned cabin, stereo music—the works. This'll be good PR, Father. When people see this, they'll know it's great to be a son of yours." Dave laid his well-muscled arm around the shaking shoulders.

Joe looked over from behind the controls and tried to ease his father's distress. "Cheer up, Father. Say, look at what this beauty can do." He grinned, gave the throttle a thrust, and spun the wheel. The boat turned in a graceful arc and headed into the waves.

"You're going the wrong way. The tide is coming. Save my children!"

"Yes, Father, we understand. Didn't we tell you? This is a lifesaving boat. We'll go in a minute. But first look at this."

The boat bounded back and forth across the waves, its powerful motor thrusting forward with thrilling power and speed. Joe executed the turns with smoothness and precision.

"No, no! Please, oh, please!" The father's anguished voice tore through the wind.

"Look at this, Father."

He could barely see the little ones now. In horror, he imagined their terror and pain. Only the tips of the rocks broke the water now. As he watched, unable to turn away, the dear, sweet heads, one by one, slipped into the waves and disappeared.

"They are gone!" Unbearable anguish ripped his body and he fell prostrate to the floor.

Then—concerned and tender hands gently cradled his frail body. "Father, we love you—please, Father . . ."

He gave no answer or indeed any sign that he had heard.

"Father, we didn't know you cared so much. We love you, Father, don't you understand? If it had been you . . ."

There was no response. Just wind and waves and—silence.

That is the passion of God. People need the Lord. Will you do what it takes to feel God's passion for the lost and actually create the changes needed to fulfill God's passion?

Notes:

1. A statement attributable to Ben Franklin rather than to Scripture.

2. George Barna, *The Index of Leading Spiritual Indicators* (Dallas: Word, 1996), 124-128.

3. Mike Regele, *Death of the Church* (Grand Rapids: Zondervan, 1995), 162.

4. Ibid., 158.

5. Barna, *Index of Leading*, 5.

6. Gen. 3:9.

7. Ex. 19:4.

8. Luke 19:10.

9. Matt. 9:13, Mark 2:17, Luke 15.

10. Luke 15:7, 10; Luke 10:17; Acts 8:8; 13:52; 15:3; 1 Thess. 2:19; Heb. 12:2.

11. Matt. 9:36; 14:14.

12. Ex. 3:7.

13. Matt. 9:37.

14. 1 Cor. 9:19-23 (New American Standard Bible).

15. Ellen G. White, *Gospel Workers* (Washington, D.C.: Review and Herald, 1945), 468; idem., *Evangelism* (Washington, D.C.: Review and Herald, 1946), 106, 70, 105; idem., *Testimonies to Ministers* (Mountain View, Calif.: Pacific Press, 1923), 251; idem., *Testimonies for the Church*, vol. 6 (Mountain View, Calif.: Pacific Press, 1948), 476, 116; Ibid., vol. 7, 25.

16. Matt. 10.

17. Christian Schwarz, *Natural Church Development* (Carol Stream, Ill.: Church Smart, 1996), 46. Schwarz' research, published in *Natural Church Development*, will be examined in detail in a later chapter.

18. Ibid., 48.

19. *Barna Report*, Jan-Feb. 1998, 1.

20. Ibid., 4.

21. Ellen G. White, *Evangelism*, 381, 382.

22. An extensive discussion of these possibilities will occur later in this book.

23. Judy Burton, *Review and Herald*, July 7, 1977.

2

Mission-driven Churches

You wake up and suddenly find that you have been transported back to the first century through the proverbial "time machine." You emerge from the time machine somewhere around A.D. 50. Your location is Antioch. You begin asking questions, seeking to find the church of Jesus there in Antioch. Finally you discover, to your astonishment, that it has no central building—instead, Christians meet in various homes.

You arrive on Sabbath morning in time for Sabbath School, but discover that there really is no Sabbath School (it wasn't invented until the nineteenth century). You look forward to the sermon, wondering which of the great apostles will deliver today's message. You soon discover, however, that there will be no sermon. There rarely is one. What happens is intriguing: members share with each other what is happening in their lives, and they talk about people with whom they have shared Christ during the week. Someone recounts that Paul and Silas were there a couple of weeks ago, and how thrilled they all are about the many new churches which these men started on their missionary journeys. Since they sent

31

Paul and Silas out from Antioch, the believers are particularly interested in hearing again what each one remembers from Paul and Silas' account.

As various people tell of their experiences, others are reminded of the sayings of Jesus that reflect what is happening in their lives, and they share those sayings together. The morning passes quickly because the members of this particular Antioch church are planning for more churches to be formed in Antioch and its vicinity. They are excited about the possibility of continually expanding the kingdom of Jesus through the new churches they will plant. Your time together is interrupted by a fellowship meal, as the believers share their bread with you around the table. They plan to spend the rest of the afternoon sharing the sayings of Jesus with some pagans who attended for the first time today.

"Wild imagination," you say. Not exactly, for the above may well describe life in the New Testament church. Scripture declares that the early believers were devoted to the apostles' teaching, fellowship, breaking of bread, and prayer.[1] You say that life in this church seems so different from church today. On the eve of the third millennium, people attend church and are passive, whereas in the first century, people in the church were active. What makes the difference? The answer is mission-driven churches.

The early church was driven by the need to fulfill the command of Jesus recorded in the Great Commission of Matthew 28:18-20. Jesus had established the church for the purpose of creating disciples in all people groups. The early church interpreted that to mean that they must establish churches everywhere. Thus the time, talent, and treasure of the church was poured into the planting of new churches. Early Christianity was truly a church planting movement.

Perhaps the best illustration of a church planting strategy in the New Testament is revealed in the life of the apostle Paul. While little is known of the exploits of the other apostles, Luke the physician carefully recorded Paul's plan and its results, thus giving us the most detailed church planting strategy of the New Testament era. One can only assume that many others operated in similar ways, for Christianity quickly became entrenched in the Roman world. For that to happen, there had to have been a strong church planting movement throughout the first hundred years of Christianity.

There is no indication in the New Testament that paid pastors were placed over the churches. Those paid for their church work were mostly church planters who devoted full time to preaching the gospel of Jesus to unreached people. Once people were evangelized, they were taught to care for themselves without a clergy person present. Then the church planter went on to start another church. Occasionally the planter would return or would write to the church to see how they were growing spiritually and numerically. When each new church had become established, it was expected to evangelize the surrounding area and start new churches there. That was life in this mission-driven church of the first century.

Could such an itinerant model of ministry still be applicable today? Would Paul's church planting strategy work in these times? Obviously, our world is greatly different from Paul's, yet in some respects it is remarkably similar. Paul was able to communicate throughout most of the Roman world in one language. There was considerable intermingling of people from different cultures in the Roman world. Society was bankrupt. Morality was loose. And a group of people, the Jews, scattered throughout the Roman world, were receptive to Paul's message.

This does not mean we should copy Paul's model slavishly, but we should examine it to see if we can build on its principles. David Hesselgrave suggests ten steps in Paul's strategy to reach the Roman world.[2] The following is an adaptation of these ten steps:

1. The church commissioned missionaries to plant churches.[3] Individuals did not go out to plant churches on their own. They were sent. Church planting is not done independently; those who plant churches are called to work in harmony with the existing church. Because all the members could not go, they sent Paul, commissioning him to go in their name. Thus Paul represented the Antioch church, and his ministry was an extension of theirs.

God does not call anyone to work independently from the body. God is leading a *movement*, and it is imperative that we all work together as we honor and appreciate one another's work:

> Our willingness to go anywhere is an intensely personal matter between us and our Master. But in order for "anywhere" to become a definite "somewhere," both our home churches and the older missionaries must have a say.[4]

First, God speaks to the person he wishes to send; then He speaks to the church to authenticate the individual's call. In our American individualism, we like to think that we can move out on our own, independent of the counsel of the wider church, but to do so is contrary to the community basis upon which New Testament life is based.

In the Adventist context, a church planter does not go out to start a church without first consulting the nearest local church and local conference. There may be resistance at times from one or both of these entities, but wisdom has proven again and again the value of following the biblical pattern of working in harmony with the existing church.

2. The church planters contacted the audience they hoped to reach.[5] Paul was the apostle to the Gentiles; yet he always began new work with Jews. Why? Because scattered throughout the Roman world were many Jewish synagogues, containing people who at least believed in the one God. They were the closest in belief to Christianity and would therefore be the most receptive people in the area. Paul knew he needed a group of local people to form the core of the new Christian company before he could begin working for the larger community.

While recognizing that Christ's message was for everyone, Paul chose to work first with those who had the least cultural differences to overcome. This plan would suggest to the modern church planter that before starting the church, they should discover who are the most receptive people in the new community. Planting churches to target certain groups of people is not only a social necessity in the twenty-first century, but has strong biblical roots in Paul's church planting strategy. It is much more difficult to plant churches cross-culturally. In the core group of new churches there should be people who are from the target group so that the cultural gap between the believers and those needing to be reached is not any wider than necessary.

3. The church planter must then seek to communicate the gospel to the receptive people.[6] Paul wasted no time. He immediately used the strategy of preaching to share the good news of Jesus with his potential audience. While there was certainly plenty of personal work on the part of Paul and his company, yet there was a strong preaching basis to their ministry. In fact, most preaching in the New Testament era was to potential new converts to Christ, rather than to existing Christians. Interestingly, this was the concept used by John Wesley, who founded the Methodist church. He would reach new people through field preaching and then organize them into classes for their growth and enrichment. Success in the various Net programs of the late 1990s indicates that preaching is still a very effective tool in reaching new people for Christ.

4. Paul did not simply present the gospel; his hearers were converted to Christ.[7] Paul called for decision and gave further instruction into the way of the gospel. Paul followed the instruction given by Jesus in the Great Commission. He saw that these people were converted to Christ and then instructed them in understanding the basics of the Christian faith. Jesus had declared that they must be taught all that He commanded. Paul obeyed.

In applying this principle to the church today, the church

planter must make certain that people have truly accepted Jesus as their Saviour and Lord. Having done so, the church planter must then provide these folk with thorough instruction into basic Christianity and give them a full understanding of the twenty-seven fundamental beliefs of the Seventh-day Adventist Church) If the church is to be Adventist, the first members must clearly understand, believe, and practice biblical Adventism. Once the new converts are solidified in the faith, they are taught to begin working with their families and friends (*oikos*) and to endeavor to bring them to Christ. That was how Paul's church's grew, and it is the way in which new churches will grow today.

5. The new believers are then organized into a church. Since the New Testament church was a community and New Testament Christianity does not envision isolated Christians independent of a body, Paul immediately brought the new believers together in the capacity of a local church[8] The initial church was probably very small—perhaps only a handful of believers who met in one home in the town) Yet it was an authentic church that was to multiply and grow.) The purpose of church fellowship is to give the new believers identity, where they can receive spiritual nourishment through the actions of a group of believers.

6. The new believers are then established in the new faith.[9] New converts will soon die if they are not rooted firmly in the faith, both doctrinally and relationally. Early Adventists would not organize a church, even though the members believed the doctrines, until they could demonstrate that they could get along relationally.[10]

To fully establish a New Testament church also meant to confirm the new body as a missionary organization and a mission-driven church. (Church planters following Paul's strategy will not leave a church until reproduction is thoroughly established in the DNA of the new church) (Reproduction is twofold: new converts are winning other new converts, and plans are being laid for the new church to start another new church). For this to happen, the church planter must spend

(significant time training the new converts for life in a missionary organization.)

**7. Leaders in the new churches were set apart and
consecrated.** [11] Amazingly, leaders were chosen very quickly
in the new churches. Leaders were not brought in from the
outside and placed over the new congregation, but were
raised up out of the harvest recently gathered. (This is a very
important step.) Selection of the wrong leader will set the
church in the wrong direction. (Therefore much prayer should
go into this process.)

If the church is to be a missionary organization, leaders
must be chosen who are committed to the missionary
mindset. (Placing into leadership a person who has never won
a soul to Jesus will result in a nonmissionary church being
established.) Therefore, the church planter should watch over
the new converts to see who are immediately reaching out
and winning new people, and also have leadership capabilities.

In Paul's model, Paul chose or appointed the leadership.
While ultimately churches will choose their own leadership,
at the beginning they may not understand the selection criteria. As a result, new churches are apt to put the wrong
people into leadership. (In the new church it is best that leadership be appointed, as Paul did, so that a missionary organization is created.) The Adventist church manual allows this.
Leaders of companies (newly planted churches) are appointed by the conference rather than being elected as they
are in the established churches. Obviously, the conference
would appoint the leader in consultation with the church
planter, who best understands who the mission-minded
people are. (Equally important today is that those selected
as leaders are doctrinally sound, teachable, and loyal to the
leadership over them.)

**8. (The church eventually reaches the place where lead-
ership is completely transferred to new leaders, and the
church planter leaves, commending the new church and
its members to the Lord.** [12]) Paul's model did not envision

a planter staying by the new church indefinitely. (The New Testament church operated on the basis of the Great Commission, which declared that people should be discipled. Once they were discipled, they were no longer to live in dependency on a preacher. In obedience to Christ, Paul discipled his converts and could then move on to establish another church.)

As we apply this principle to the church today, we will need to teach churches to care for themselves. Since all "care" passages in the New Testament are addressed to all members, who are to provide mutual care for each other, (this concept should be a necessity for all mission-driven, New Testament, community-based churches.) We will also need to teach the new church how to carry on its services in the absence of clergy, or if clergy are present, not to depend on the clergy.

9. After Paul left the area, he continued a relationship with the churches he had founded. [13] Paul did not neglect the new churches. He trusted the leadership he had appointed, but periodically he communicated with the church through letter or personal visit. Often major problems developed, such as at Corinth, and Paul needed to give counsel that would help the newly planted church solve their problems. The church planters will usually have a bond forever with the churches they have founded, so that counsel can be given even after the planter has moved on to other churches.

This part of Paul's strategy is difficult for us today, because our usual procedure is to place a pastor over the new church, and the planter is to stay out. However, (this step in Paul's strategy is essential as we establish non-pastor-dependent churches or churches without pastors) Problems will develop that will need special attention. The church planter will be the ideal person to come back for a visit and help the church through the difficulty. In our modern age of mass communication, the planter can be only an e-mail away.

10. New churches became a part of the sisterhood of

churches and sent representatives to the various councils of the church.[14] While there is no formal evidence that new churches in the New Testament era were inducted into a sisterhood of churches, there is evidence that the churches were interrelated. This is seen by the fact that the newly founded churches sent representatives to the Jerusalem council and that Paul reported back to the churches that sent him. This clearly reveals an interdependence of each church with the other Christian churches.

In the work of the church today, new churches are not to be left to themselves. Just as Christians live in mutual dependence upon one another; so each church lives in mutual dependence upon every other church. We may be separate congregations, but we are one body in Christ. Just as all the early churches were expected to accept and follow the recommendations of the Jerusalem council, so the Church today realizes that all churches respect the decisions made by representatives from all the various churches. That is why General Conference decisions in session carry such weight in the Seventh-day Adventist Church. They do not possess biblical authority, but they do carry the highest ecclesiastical authority among us. Such authority is harmonious with the New Testament era. Congregationalism is totally foreign to the community basis of the New Testament church. The early church was an interrelated church.

A Case Study[15]

The above ten points are reflective of Paul's overall church planting strategy. Acts 16 gives us a more detailed account of how Paul specifically established the church at Philippi. Verses 1-5 indicate that Paul had selected young Timothy as a member of his church planting team at this time. Paul was both strengthening previously planted churches, and moving on to Philippi to establish a new plant.

Paul probably chose Timothy deliberately because he was a native of the area, and thus culturally close to the people they were trying to reach. Timothy underwent circumcision, even though he did not have to, because Paul's strategy involved beginning with Jewish people who would have been offended by an uncircumcised person among them. In following Paul's example, church planting teams today should be composed of people who are culturally similar to the people being targeted. (If ability, character, and spirituality are equal in two leaders, but one is closer to the targeted group culturally, the one nearest culturally should always be chosen.) Most New Testament planting was done in teams, because of the community understanding of the church. There was no individualistic church planting in the New Testament. The value of a church planting team is that there is a better chance of one person on the team being culturally relevant.

Not only was Paul trying to be culturally relevant, but he was also in touch with the Spirit. In one instance when he planned to go one direction, the Spirit sent him somewhere else.[16] The amazing thing is that Paul was so in tune with the Spirit that he was willing to change his plans to go where the Spirit led. (Church planters today need to be in tune with the Spirit.) They need to spend significant time with God in prayer and Bible study so that they hear the voice of the Spirit speaking to them. Then they must obey the voice. (The secret of success in church planting is to find a place where the Spirit is already working and then follow.) We need to learn to ride the wave of God's Spirit.

One of the things church planters learn very quickly is that things do not always go as they had envisioned. While we need to plan well, we must be willing to change our plans as the Spirit directs. (Church planting never goes quite the way we think it will.)

The Spirit led Paul and his church planting team to Philippi, a new town unknown to Paul and his team.[17] Interestingly, Paul did not immediately plunge into preaching. It was several days before he made his first contact. We are not told what he did in the interim. Perhaps he just rested, but more likely he was getting acquainted with the town so that he would understand how to reach the people. He evidently learned that there was a place of worship out by the riverside where some women gathered each Sabbath. Thus, that would be a good place to begin. Following this example, the church planter today will learn as much as possible about the place where the church will be planted. We have sophisticated data-gathering mechanisms that enable us to analyze and dissect a city before we enter it.[18] (Today's planter will also attempt, as did Paul, to begin with those who are the closest culturally.)

As Paul preached there by the riverside, Lydia responded to the message of salvation, and Paul quickly followed through by working for her and her household.[19] Soon they were all baptized, and an embryonic church was born. Lydia responded so quickly, one can only conclude that she and her household were experiencing deep spiritual hunger and were searching for truth. (The church planter today will need to concentrate on those in whom the Spirit has already awakened a spiritual hunger.)

Paul won not only Lydia, but her whole *oikos* (household).[20] (Along with each new convert, church planters will need to evangelize the networks of people they know.) The early church grew rapidly because it spread through the natural networks of people associated with the new converts. Each person who comes to Christ has many friends, relatives, and associates who could easily be led to the Lord and to the church if we follow Paul's example.

As soon as Lydia was converted, she invited Paul and the team to stay at her home.[21] Paul and the team accepted the hospitality offered. They were not afraid to accept the gifts of the new converts. The resources for the new church are in the harvest. New churches should not be subsidized for long periods of time, as this practice creates dependency. (The churches need to learn very quickly to care for themselves financially.) Churches that are continually subsidized are weak. We in Adventism need to find a way to avoid sustained financial sponsorship of a church, even in pastoral coverage. It is permissible when the new church is getting started, but quickly the subsidy needs to end; the new church must become financially independent and begin contributing to the formation of other new churches. Church planting should not be a costly matter. It only becomes so when we insist on subsidizing the pastoral coverage and constructing a building. The resources are in the harvest. A church that is continually reaching out will find all the resources it needs in the harvest without continually depending on other churches for their support.

The first convert in Europe was a woman. Do not discount the value of women in church planting. Most new churches are built around relationships, and women are usually better adapted to building relationships than are men. Therefore, they are extremely important to the success of the church plant in its initial stages.

Acts 16:16 indicates that Paul and his team continually met at the place of prayer. Prayer was a vital part of Paul's church planting program. And the converts were introduced to prayer time, as well. The key ingredient for successful church planting is prayer. Surveys of successful church planters indicate that they felt the most essential ingredient in church planting was a life of prayer.

Church planting is spiritual warfare. Church planters fight the devil as does no one else, because they are invading Satan's territory. He does not give up without a struggle. Verses 16-18 of Acts reveal demonic activity for the purpose of casting negative reflection on Paul and his team publicly. Church planters should not be surprised when the enemy attacks. Verses 19-25 indicate that the team handled the opposition well. Even when falsely accused, they did not complain. They went to prison rejoicing. Church planters can expect opposition, but the way they handle that opposition may well determine their success or failure as church planters. Church planters need to be big enough to recognize that God is leading in spite of the opposition. It is easy to become whiners, but a mark of maturity is the ability to ac-

cept tribulations and trials with joy. Church planters need X
mature faith.)

In the midst of adversity, church planters can expect God
to intervene for His glory.[22] Through the mighty earthquake,
God was able to rouse the jailer to his sense of need. As a
result, he literally cried out to God for help. God heard, and
the jailer found the peace of Christ. God seems to work
greater miracles to reach the heathen than He performs for
those who are already His followers. The jailer became the
first European convert from heathenism.

Since miracles in Scripture seem to have taken place primarily when new work was being started,/church planters   X
should expect miracles from God to help them in the establishment of new churches) This does not mean that church
planters should attempt to manufacture a miracle, but they
should not be surprised when God performs miracles to
advance His kingdom.

Not only was the jailer's interest aroused, but he actually
gave his life to Christ, along with his whole *oikos*.[23] The jailer
was an unlikely candidate for the church. Roman soldiers
were not known for their religious devotion. Paul had every
reason to hate the jailer. After all, he had imprisoned Paul,
placed him in stocks, and probably had made his life miserable. Paul's humanity would have said, "Let him take his own
life." Paul, however, saw even in the jailer a potential convert.

(Church planters need "kingdom eyes." They need to see X
everyone they meet as a potential candidate for the new
church and for the kingdom of God. The biggest opponents
to the church plant may well be some of the first members,
just as at Philippi.)

A pastor one time responded to an ad for a used refrigerator. The pastor could have spent his time arguing the merits
or demerits of the refrigerator with the seller, but because
the pastor had "kingdom eyes," he saw the seller as a potential candidate for the kingdom of God. As a result, he not

only bought the refrigerator but also arranged Bible studies. A few months later he baptized the man and his family. Church planters need to see converts everywhere.

Imagine the hours that Paul put in that day. From the time of his arrest to the time he was expelled from the city, he was awake and working. It probably was close to forty straight hours filled with stress, tension, euphoria, and despair. Church planters can expect to put in long days with a lot of stress and plenty of highs and lows.(To do church planting requires hard work, long hours, disrupted schedules and high risk.) But it is worth it all for the sake of the kingdom. After all, Jesus put in hard work, long hours, and high risk to save us. Shouldn't church planters be willing to do the same?

The amazing truth is that to establish the church at Philippi, Paul actually allowed himself to be imprisoned and tortured. He could have saved himself the trouble if he had only claimed his rights at the beginning. Instead, he waited until after the conversion of the jailer before he informed the authorities that he was a Roman citizen.[24] If he had claimed his rights at the beginning, the jailer would not have been won to Christ. Of course, Paul did not know that ahead of time. But sometimes it may be best for the church planter not to claim his rights too quickly.

When one is persecuted unjustly, it arouses sympathy among those who see the planter as willing to suffer unjustly for the cause of Christ. Ultimately the gain is seen when many people come to Christ because the planter has not claimed his rights too quickly. Today one can expect opposition from civil authorities who do not want valuable property off the tax roles or from other churches who don't want a new church competing with them. There is a time to claim your rights, but it may be best to wait out the situation for awhile. God can use the opposition aroused to bring new people to faith, just as He did with the jailer.

Paul was not granted the privilege of staying for a long time in Philippi, he had to leave immediately. But he first got the little church together and encouraged them.[25] Then he left, and entrusted them with the gospel, and the church at Philippi grew. Paul had laid the foundation well, and, as we mentioned earlier, he trusted the leadership he raised up to continue the work he had started. He did not choose leadership from outside the newly established church. He had started a truly indigenous church.

> A church that must depend on foreigners for its workers, that must call for additional missionaries to extend the work . . . is not an indigenous church. It is a hot-house plant that must have an artificial atmosphere and receive special care to keep alive . . . Surely the weak thing we have produced is not what Jesus meant when He said, "I will build my church and the gates of hell shall not prevail against it.[26]

Paul was the master church planter of the New Testament era. Examining his strategy, we have discovered many principles that are applicable to church planting today. In later chapters we will seek to put these principles to work in forming a strategy for church planting in our day. Our study in this chapter has revealed church planting to be at the heart and center of New Testament Christianity. In fact, the early church was a church planting movement. The whole church was organized to facilitate church planting as its primary function. That was because the New Testament church was a Great Commission church. Jesus had told them to do this, and they simply followed and did it. Why don't we do the same?

Notes:

1. Acts 2:42.

2. David Hesselgrave, *Planting Churches Cross Culturally* (Grand Rapids: Baker, 1980).

3. Acts 13:1-4; 15:39, 40.

4. Michael C. Griffiths, *You and God's Work Overseas* (Chi-

cago: InterVarsity Press, 1967), 21.

5. Acts 13:14-16; 14:1.

6. Acts 13:16-41.

7. Acts 13:48; 16:14, 15.

8.See the author's work, *The Revolutionized Church of the 21st Century* (Fallbrook, CA: Hart Research, 1997).

9. Acts 14:21, 22; 15:41.

10.Loughborough, *The Church: Its Organization*, 126.

11. Acts. 14:23.

12. Acts 14:23; 16:40.

13. Acts 15:36; 18:23

14. Acts 14:26, 27; 15:1-4.

15.Some of the ideas in this section have been adapted from Charles Chaney, *Church Planting at the End of the Twentieth Century* (Wheaton, Il.: Tyndale, 1991).

16. Acts 16:6-10.

17. Acts 16:11, 12.

18. Resources for data gathering will be considered in a later chapter.

19. Acts 16:13-15.

20. Acts 16:15.

21. Ibid.

22. Acts 16:25-30.

23. Acts 16:31-34.

24. Acts 16:35-39.

25. Acts 16:40.

26.Melvin L. Hodges, *The Indigenous Church* (Springfield, Mo.: Gospel Publishing House, 1952), 17, 18.

3

The Rebirth of a Church Planting Movement: Early Adventism

It was perhaps a bright, sunny day in that New England autumn, with colorful leaves sparkling in the brilliant sunlight on that October day as believers in the advent entered upon what they felt was their last day on planet Earth. But the day that began with such bright promise became one of bitter disappointment as these early believers had to face instead the gray cold of another bitter New England winter. Christ had not come and they had to endure a scoffing world.

Following the "great disappointment," most Millerites joined the fledgling Advent Christian church, which numbered some fifty thousand at its organization in 1849.[1] However, another group refused to believe that Miller's dates were wrong or that his method of calculating the time prophecy of Daniel 8:14 was in error. These early believers spent the years between 1844 and 1850 in various Bible conferences, hammering out a system of clear biblical truth. In contrast to the fifty thousand who became first-day Adventists, this almost unnoticeable group numbered less than three hundred in 1849, the smallest of all the groups arising from the Millerite movement. This is the group which eventually became the Seventh-day Adventist Church.

Having discovered a clear line of biblical truth, the believers finally began to realize that this great message of biblical truth must be shared with the world. From this humble beginning they began to share the heart of their message: Christ in the heavenly sanctuary and Christ in the Sabbath. Today their descendants number more than ten million. How did this happen? Solely because those early Adventist pioneers realized that their church was to be a mission-driven church. Only thus could the world be won to the glorious truths they had discovered in God's Word. As a result, their whole organization was designed to support a church in mission. All that the church did was centered around the fulfillment of the mission which they felt God had called them to fulfill.

As a church ages, it has a tendency to lose sight of the vision that propelled it in its early days. Other things take the place of that which should be the church's top priority. These things are good, and many times are the means to fulfill the church's mission, but sometimes they become an end in themselves, with the ultimate result that the church no longer majors in its mission.

Churches go through a life cycle similar to that of human beings. A church, for example, has a normal life cycle of sixty to seventy years, although a few, like humans, become centurions. Most churches actually stop growing by the time they reach their fifteenth birthday, hold a plateau for twenty to thirty years, and then enter a period of slow decline. After being on a plateau for several years, a church is actually on the downside of its life cycle.

The first stage of this downside is nostalgia, as a church begins to reminisce about its past. During this stage individuals will recall the "good old days" when Pastor Jones was here. From nostalgia the church moves to a period of questioning, when people begin to question why things are not the way they used to be. From there the church moves to polarization, where warring camps develop, and finally the church self destructs as death sets in.

The frightening thought is that the Adventist church in North America resembles more and more the characteristics of the downside of the life cycle. But the Adventist church *must not* self destruct. God has higher plans for this church than that. Dr. Robert D. Dale, in his book *To Dream Again,* suggests that a church on the downside of the life cycle must go back and rebirth its dream.[2] The rebirthing of the dream is the only way out of the self destruction that lies ahead if we continue on the downside of our life cycle as a denomination.

Dr. Robert Logan, a church planting consultant who addressed the first two sessions of the Adventist Church's *Seeds* conferences on church planting, made clear to Adventists that the solution to our problem lies in our history. He told the convention that we need to go back to our roots and discover what made us a mighty movement of God in the beginning. In the history of our early days we will find the solution to the stagnant life of most Adventist churches at the beginning of the twenty-first century.

In this chapter we wish to reexamine those early Adventists who had discovered the truth of the sanctuary and the Sabbath and discover how they organized their church for the accomplishment of the mission God gave them. From that understanding we will be able to formulate a plan that will enable us to develop a mission-driven church once again.

Early Adventist Organization

Organization was something feared by most early Adventists. Having been thrown out of their churches, most of them were reluctant to immediately organize themselves into a church. However, under the guidance of James and Ellen White, and in view of the necessity of the church to own property, they reluctantly organized in 1863. In so doing, they tried to follow the counsel of the New Testament and to create a church that was organized in a radically different way from that of other denominations.

Theirs was to be a mission-driven church. Therefore the structure had to support the mission. Organization was not to control (which was what they feared). Organization was to facilitate the accomplishment of the mission. Mission was primary. Everything else in the church was subservient to mission. Time, talent, and treasure were only of use for the furtherance of the mission of the church.

J. N. Loughborough, early church historian, quotes a document that he declares was used in the organization of the General Conference.[3] In that document the early Adventists leaders sought to create a mission organization. They declared that the Scriptures recognized only two kinds of church officers: those called by God—the apostles and the evangelists, and those appointed by the church—the elders, the deacons, and the pastors. The first two positions they held to be clergy positions; the last three they declared to be local and lay positions.[4] The amazing thing is that early Adventists actually regarded the pastoral role as a local lay position and not a clergy position. The result was that they developed a system where clergy were primarily church planters and evangelists. Local churches, once planted, were taught to care for themselves, while the clergy were free to continue planting new churches. Local churches were entrusted to local, unpaid lay elders.

Churches sent their tithe to the conference to support the clergy who were raising up new churches, not to support local pastors. In their view, local churches did not need a pastor. Instead, all the tithe could be available to support a church planting movement, for that was what they saw themselves to be. No church was clamoring for their share of the tithe. Since the entire membership had a mission mindset, the members were willing to provide for their own care in order that more people might hear the message. (Evangelism and church planting were the top priority of the early Adventist church.) The system that we have inherited, whereby the tithe is paid to the conference, comes from a time when that system supported a church planting movement. Today the tithe supports local pastors caring for local churches, something that would have been anathema to these early Adventist pioneers with their understanding of church mission .

Nowhere is this mission mentality more obvious than in the role given to clergy during the first sixty years of Adventist history. Even the hiring of the first clergy in the fledgling Adventist church arose out of a need for mission rather than a need for nurture. Loughborough again describes the reason for the need of clergy:

> In the summer of 1854, Seventh-day Adventists first began to use large tents in which to hold meetings. It was a rare thing in those days to see tents used for such a purpose; consequently crowds of people came to the tent meetings.

> This increased interest in the message called for ministers who could devote their whole time to gospel work. This they could not do without some means of support besides their own hand labor.[5]

Mission was the driving force of the church during this time. (Preachers were hired, not to preach to Adventists, but to reach new believers and start new churches. All Adventists preachers cut their eye teeth in church planting.) James White indicated that if a person could not plant a church, he had no right to assume that God had called him to preach the third angel's message·

> In no way can a preacher so well prove himself as in entering new fields. There he can see the fruits of his own labors. And if he be successful in raising up churches, and establishing them, so that they

bear good fruits, he gives to his brethren the best proofs that he is sent of the Lord.[6]

Some who join the Seventh-day Adventists commence at once to preach to the brethren, many of whom are far in advance of them. And our brethren often err in urging such to spend their time in preaching to them. Let such ministers first be suitably instructed by those of experience in the message, then let them go out into new fields, trusting God for help and success. And when they shall have raised up churches, and shall have properly instructed them, then those churches will support them. If they cannot raise up churches and friends to sustain them, then certainly the cause of truth has no need of them, and they have the best reasons for concluding that they made a sad mistake when they thought that God called them to teach the third angel's message.[7]

Thus, for the first fifty to sixty years of its history the Adventist church existed without "settled pastors" over churches. Even the denomination's largest church, in Battle Creek, operated without a paid pastor. James White did serve as pastor for a few years, but at the same time he was also president of the General Conference, head of the publishing work, and in charge of the medical work. His work as pastor was his contribution to the local church where he belonged. In other words, he served as the local elder in charge of pastoring the church.

The result of this commitment to mission is obvious in the fantastic growth of Adventism in the nineteenth century. Since this was the main activity of most Adventist pastors, churches were planted at amazing rates. For example, in the 1870s a new church was planted each year for every two ordained ministers. This was sustained for all ten years of the decade. In the 1880s, the rate was for every five or six ordained ministers, and in the 1890s, one new church was established every year for every four ordained ministers.

Today, in the first half of the 1990s, more than one hundred and twenty pastors are required to raise up one church each year in North America.

If modern Adventist pastors were to plant churches at the same rate as their forefathers, North America today would be planting 1,822 churches a year by the 1870s rate; or 629 a year by the 1880s rate; or 768 a year by the 1890s rate. Instead, in the first half of the 1990s, North American Adventists had only 25 to 30 new starts. Since the beginning of the *Seeds* Conferences, however, that has increased to around 12.5 per month, or 150 a year as we near the end of the decade.[8] The difference between then and now is a mission organization and a church planting movement. Fortunately, the North American church is beginning to return to being a church planting movement, but we still have a long way to go.

With no localized clergy but an itinerant ministry constantly planting new churches, early Adventists allocated the majority of their resources to reaching the harvest. They were a mission organization, and mission organizations are always involved in mission. They knew no other way to do church. As a result, throughout the nineteenth century Adventism had no settled pastors, but focused entirely on planting new churches. The pioneers claimed that was the reason for their rapid growth during that era:

THE SEVENTH-DAY ADVENTISTS

Some Facts and Figures Gathered from Elder Starr—How They Have Grown in Forty Years—and What They Believe

"By what means have you carried forward your work so rapidly?"

"Well, in the first place," replied the Elder, "we have no settled pastors. Our churches are taught to take care of themselves, while nearly all of our ministers work as evangelists in new fields. In the winter they go out into the churches, halls, or school houses and raise up believers. In the summer we use tents, pitching them in the cities and villages where we teach the people these doctrines."[9]

The Seventh-day Baptists agreed that this itinerant church planting model was the reason that Adventist growth was surpassing their growth by the turn of the century.

All Seventh-day Adventist clergymen are missionaries—not located pastors—and are busy preaching, teaching, and organizing churches the world over.[10]

Early Adventists indeed considered themselves a church in mission. The constant emphasis for the church was evangelism and church planting. Each year the clergy from the state conference would gather together to examine the calls that had come for starting up new work. Having examined the calls, the clergy would retire to their room to pray, asking God to guide their decision as to where they should go that year to raise up churches. Having prayed it through they would return to the room and announce where they felt God was calling. Inevitably, a new church would be born in that location during the next year. A. G. Daniells as late as 1912 warned the church that if they abandoned this model of ministry, the church would die.

We have not settled our ministers over churches as pastors to any large extent. In some of the very large churches we have elected pastors, but as a rule we have held ourselves ready for field service, evangelistic work and our brethren and sisters have held themselves ready to maintain their church services and carry forward their church work without settled pastors. And I hope this will never cease to be the order of affairs in this denomination; for when we cease our forward movement work and begin to settle over our churches, to stay by them, and do their thinking and their praying and their work that is to be done, then our churches will begin to weaken, and to lose their life and spirit, and become paralyzed and fossilized and our work will be on a retreat.[11]

Clearly this mission mindset was not just a passing fad. It was not simply an organizational structure erected because the churches were small and few, but rather it was a structure created to serve a church in mission, a church that viewed itself primarily as a church planting movement. Ellen White also gave her ringing endorsement to this model of ministry. In fact, her influence was so strong in this direction that as long as she was alive and A. G. Daniells was president of the General Conference, this model of pastoral role remained intact. However, by 1920 Daniells was out of the presidency and Ellen White's voice was silent. The protest against abandoning this model of ministry had lost its two chief exponents.

During the first twenty years of the twentieth century, cries were made to have pastors over churches, but Ellen White and Daniells were firmly against it. With their demise, nothing could stem the tide. Pastors were quickly placed over churches throughout North America. The result was a rapid drop in church planting and a slowing of the evangelistic advance of the church.

Ellen White and Settled Pastors

With the cry echoing throughout North America to have settled pastors, Ellen White could not be silent. She emphatically endorsed the itinerant model and urged the church not to abandon it. Ellen White clearly understood the Adventist church to be a church planting movement:

> As churches are established, it should be set before them that it is even from among them that men must be taken to carry the truth to others, and raise up new churches; therefore they must all work, and cultivate to the utmost the talents that God has given them, and be training their minds to engage in the service of their Master.[12]

Do not depend on the ministers to do all the work in your church and neighborhood. The pastors must seek the lost sheep, and you must help them; and while the ministers are called to labor in other parts of the vineyard, the people of God must have light in themselves, speaking to each other in psalms and hymns and spiritual songs, singing with grace in our hearts and making melody unto the Lord. While you should respect the ministers highly for their work's sake, you must not trust them as your saviors, but build yourselves up in the most holy faith. When you assemble in the house of God, tell your experiences, and you will grow stronger. While you speak in meeting, you are gaining an education that will enable you to labor for others.[13]

Ellen White's position is clear. The clergy are church planters, seeking the "lost sheep" while they leave the flock safely in the fold to care for themselves. Ellen White could not envision the need of a pastor to look after a church. To do so would admit that the church had not fully done its work in discipling the new converts. In her view, any church that had to depend on a minister was not yet fully evangelized. Instead, the early Adventist congregations cared for themselves as did their counterparts of the first century, by maintaining their services without the "benefit" of clergy. In place of a preaching service, they shared their experience. The sharing of one's Christian life had a more profound impact upon Christian growth than a sermon ever could.

Another factor is indicated in the above quotation. The weekly sharing of their experience in church prepared the believers to share their experience as witnesses outside of church. Since the weekly service for most Adventists at the beginning of the twenty-first century is one of passivity in church, it should not be surprising that most Adventists are passive in their witness outside of church. In fact, this failure to make the sharing of one's faith a regular part of worship may be one of the main reasons for the general lack of witness on the part of most North American Adventists.[14] This is why Ellen White urged that Adventists should not expect a sermon every Sabbath:

> It has often been presented to me that there should be less sermonizing by ministers acting merely as local pastors of churches, and that greater personal efforts should be put forth. Our people should not be made to think that they need to listen to a sermon every Sabbath. Many who listen frequently to sermons, even though the truth be preached in clear lines, learn but little. Often it would be more profitable if the Sabbath meetings were of the same nature as a Bible class study.[15]

As calls began to rise for settled pastors during the first two decades of the twentieth century, Ellen White increased the volume as she endorsed the church planting configuration that had guided the Adventist church for over fifty years:

> There should not be a call to have settled pastors over our churches, but let the life-giving power of the truth impress the individual members to act, leading them to labor interestedly to carry on efficient missionary work in each locality. As the hand of God, the church is to be educated and trained to do effective service. Its members are to be the Lord's devoted Christian workers.[16]

She could not have made her point any plainer than she did here. Not only should the Adventist church not have settled pastors, but there should not even be a call issued to have them. Ellen White clearly understood that the organization which they had created was to be mission-centered, and she was not about to stand idly by as its mission was destroyed. The Adventist church was not created to copy other Protestant denominations; it was unique. It was to be forever a church in mission, giving the last warning message to the world. It was to keep reaching out, annexing new territories until it had engulfed the entire world.) Therefore, the Adventist church was to be organized differently from other denominations. It was to be organized to support a church planting movement, and it was to be a mission organization, (not an organization to babysit existing Adventists, who should have the spiritual maturity to exist on their own without a settled pastor over them.)

> God calls for pastors and teachers and evangelists. (From door to door His servants are to proclaim the gospel message.) The knowledge of present truth is not to lead those who receive it to settle down and colonize; it is to lead them into new places.[17] Reproduce

Some may feel that our denomination has matured since those early days, that because we have large churches today, they need a pastor over them; our times are different. However, there were large churches in early Adventism, such as at Battle Creek, and that church received some of the strongest condemnations from the pen of Ellen White for its dependency on the workers who lived in Battle Creek, instead of having life in itself.

However, Ellen White's reason for insistence on this model of the pastoral role was twofold. We have already noted her church planting rationale and her commitment to the Adventist church's mission. (Her other concern was for the health of the church.) It was her strong feeling that churches with pastors were weak and lifeless, and that churches would be more healthy spiritually if they did not have a settled pastor. Her fear was that settled pastorates would create weak Christians.

> Forgetting that strength to resist evil is best gained by aggressive service, they began to think that they had no work so important as that of shielding the church in Jerusalem from the attacks of the enemy. Instead of educating the new converts to carry the gospel to those who had not heard it, they were in danger of taking a course that would

lead all to be satisfied with what had been accomplished. To scatter His representatives abroad, where they could work for others, (God permitted persecution to come upon them.) Driven from Jerusalem, the believers "went everywhere preaching the word."

Those who would be overcomers must be drawn out of themselves, and the only thing which will accomplish this great work, (is to become intensely interested in the salvation of others.[18])

(It is clear from her pen that as churches work in the harvest, they grow spiritually, but as churches concentrate on their own needs and problems, they weaken and decay.) This general philosophy is further stated by Ellen White as follows:

> God has not given His ministers the work of setting the churches right. No sooner is this work done, apparently, than it has to be done over again. Church members that are thus looked after and labored for become religious weaklings. If nine tenths of the effort that has been put forth for those who know the truth had been put forth for those who have never heard the truth, how much greater would have been the advancement made!
>
> Sometimes ministers do too much; they seek to embrace the whole work in their arms. It absorbs and dwarfs them; yet they continue to grasp it all. They seem to think that they alone are to work in the cause of God, while the members of the church stand idle. This is not God's order at all.
>
> (The greatest help that can be given our people is to teach them to work for God, and to depend on Him, not on the ministers.)
>
> So long as church members make no effort to give others the help given them, great spiritual feebleness must result.[19]

In Ellen White's view, pastoral dependency creates weak churches and immature church members. This view of pastoral dependency persisted for some time after the church abandoned its mission-centered understanding of the pastoral role. H.M.S. Richards, Sr., reminiscing about this earlier time, declared that when he started in the ministry, churches that needed a pastor were looked upon as being decadent:

> Then he [F. E. Wilcox] went on to write about something which I suppose is hard for some of us today to understand and feel about as he did. He mentioned what he called the "unfortunate growing tendency in our denomination toward settled pastorates." The time of too many of our preachers, instead of being occupied with carrying the message into new fields, is taken up in settling church difficulties and laboring for men and women who should be towers of strength instead of subjects for labor.
>
> When I was baptized, and later became a young preacher, we looked upon churches that had to have settled pastors over every flock as being decadent. Most of our preachers were out on the firing line, holding meetings, winning men to Christ, and raising up new churches. Then every few months they would come around and visit the churches that had already been established. This seemed to be, according to our view of it, the plan of the apostolic church.[20]

Decadent churches if they needed a pastor? How strange that sounds to our ears today, when we have become so accustomed to having our pastors doing everything in many of our churches. As pastors were hired to care for the churches, both spirituality and evangelism declined, and church planting took a real back seat. Having pastors over churches has not worked in the Seventh-day Adventist Church. This model of the pastoral role needs to be relegated to the history book as a failed enterprise. We need to discover a new paradigm.

Actually, having the pastor as the shepherd of the flock is a ministry model that dates back some sixteen hundred years. The seeds for this were sown during the second century, and it was fully implemented in the fourth. After the conversion of Constantine, the entire Roman empire became Christian. There was no longer a need for an evangelizing clergy and membership, since everyone in the empire was Christian. Evangelism became the responsibility of the professional soldiers who went into distant lands and conquered new territory for the empire, thus making those lands Christian.

The job of clergy got reassigned to the care of existing members who were now grouped into parishes. Gone was the mission understanding of church. The result was the Dark Ages.[21] However, today we no longer live in the Middle Ages where the whole world is Christian. We live in a world that desperately needs evangelization. If for no other reason than that, we need to return to a mission understanding of church and abandon what became the Catholic model of clergy role in the Dark Ages.

(Again, Ellen White's concern was for the church to fully disciple people.) She considered the need of a pastor to care for the congregation to be evidence that people had not been discipled, and therefore the church needed to be reconverted.

> The churches are dying and they want a minister to preach to them. They should be taught to bring a faithful tithe to God, that He may strengthen and bless them: they should be brought into working order, that the breath of God may come into them. They should be taught that unless they can stand alone, without a minister, they need to be converted anew, and baptized anew. They need to be born again.[22]

Ellen White could not have been more emphatic. This was no passing fad. The very life of the church was at stake.

Churches that could not exist without a pastor were decadent—they needed to be worked with as new converts and educated for self sufficiency so they could stand on their own without a pastor.

Settled Pastors in the Early Twentieth Century

Even though Ellen White clearly advocated that God's primary design for the Adventist church was that there be no settled pastors, the church began to place pastors over the larger churches during the first twenty years of the twentieth century. She continued to present the ideal, but also suggested that when pastors were placed over churches, they should evangelize and train, but not do the work which the believers should be doing. Much of her counsel dealing with the pastor as a trainer stems from this time period. But at the same time she strongly urged that pastors were not to hover over the churches that know the truth, but instead were to be out seeking the lost sheep. Some pastors reacted against Ellen White's strong appeal by stating that even though they were settled over churches, they were not hovering over them. One who reacted at the 1901 General Conference Session was J. O. Corliss, pastor of the San Francisco church:

> A man can hover over, and simply preach to a church until it depends entirely upon his preaching; but our church does not do that. Our church is at work. We try to get every member of the church at work. But the pastor wants to have a discriminating mind, as he talks with different members of the church, to know just what that individual is fitted for. I believe we can do this.[23]

He then proceeds to describe what his church is doing. They were holding services on the first and third Sundays of every month in the Seaman's home. In addition, they had a jail ministry on the third Sunday of every month. A health talk was held every Thursday night. Members were reaching out to the poor of the city, sharing healthful living as well as food and clothing with them. At times they were able to talk to them about Jesus. Groups of people were visiting the sick and the elderly. Members sold over two hundred and fifty *Signs* magazines every month, and were even carrying on a Japanese and Chinese work in the city. One can readily see that the church was not pastor dependent.

> All these committees report at the regular weekly workers' meetings. I have little else to do in these plans of work than to counsel with those engaged in carrying them out. This much seems necessary where so many are engaged in work, in order to preserve harmony and unity of purpose.[24]

He then reported that they had baptisms every month, but that he deserved no credit for them since all he did was to facilitate the members' ministries. They did all the work.

One has to admit that this is not hovering. Yet this is Ellen White's second choice and not the ideal. But even this bears faint resemblance to today's church.

What Are We To Do?

Can we replicate the nineteenth century Adventist model of church planting at the beginning of the twenty-first century? Obviously not. To do so would be a sad mistake. Times are different. However, we must be willing to extract the principles from the early Adventist model and endeavor to implement those principles in the way we do church today. What are those principles?

The basic principle is to have a mission-centered organization. Whatever the structure of the local church, it must be mission-centered. Second, churches must not be pastor-dependent. Care of existing congregations should not consume the majority of the time of clergy. Thirdly, people must be discipled and trained so that they can stand on their own. This is simply a question of church health. Churches that are dependent on clergy to do all their work for them are not healthy.)

Any model for church planting needs to be based on these principles. This author suggests four possible models that could be in harmony with the principles enunciated above. That does not mean there are only four ways to do it. Other models are possible, but the four explored below can form a beginning.

Model One: The Traditional Church

Many have pronounced the traditional church as passé, but it has proved quite resilient, and will probably be around for some time. By *traditional church* is meant a church over whom a settled pastor presides. However, while the basic form will remain intact, there will need to be some serious adjustments to this model in order for it to successfully fulfill Christ's mission in the twenty-first century.

The biggest adjustment will need to be in the role of the pastor. Traditionally, most Adventist churches have seen their pastor as the chief caregiver of the church. Instead, the role will need to be adjusted so that the main focus of the pastor becomes training and equipping the saints for ministry. Rather than performing ministry, the pastor's chief role will become facilitating the ministry of the laity. This would be in harmony with the job description found in Ephesians 4:11, 12.[25] In this context, the pastor's function would be much like that of Adventist Pastor J. O. Corliss in San Francisco at the beginning of the twentieth century. Rather than hovering over the churches, the pastor would be facilitating and coordinating the ministries of the laity in the church.

This model is needed because of some peoples' expectations that a church should have a pastor. Many of Adventism's churches could not exist without this model of church. Even when churches see the value of the early Adventist paradigm, (it is difficult for them to change.)Making these adjustments enables them to be in harmony with the principles enunciated by Scripture and Ellen White. Because of the wider expectations in the world, Adventism will need to continue to function with these kinds of churches in order to attract people who have these expectations.

Many new churches will also need to be planted in this model. During the latter part of the twentieth century, the seeker-sensitive model of church planting has been very popular with many. The seeker-sensitive type church would be one example of a church planted in this model. Any communities that have a high view of the pastor, such as the African-American community, will need to continue planting churches in this model in order to reach their target groups.

Existing churches will need to be educated and then transitioned to this new understanding of pastoral role. In no area will this be more difficult than in the area of clergy care. Most congregations have become accustomed to receiving care from the clergy. To receive such care from the laity instead may be difficult for some. The wise pastor who wishes to transition to this model will slowly move the church toward this goal. Rather than take away care, the pastor will work intelligently by talking to the membership about increasing care and facilitating lay care, while at the same time continuing regular clergy care. As the church becomes accustomed to this new level of better care, the pastor can slowly ease out of the heavy load of pastoral care and free time up for evangelism. Even newly planted churches will need education and training in this area, before this practice is fully established in the new church.

One of the ways to increase the amount of care by members for one another is to solicit the help of lay volunteers who will come to the church once a month and call other members to see how they are doing spiritually. Any potential problems spotted could be passed on to the pastor or the elders for follow up. If all members receive a call from the church each month just to ask about their spiritual well being, it will provide members with far more care than they expect under the present program and will diminish criticism of the church for not providing the same level of clergy care.)What this model calls for is not less care, but more. To accomplish that, we can no longer depend on the clergy alone;(we need to involve the whole membership in the caring process.)

This model will function primarily with churches that have around one hundred and fifty or more in attendance. Many such churches will need multiple staff members in order to function adequately, even in a model of nondependency. One of Adventism's current problems is the inability to provide adequate staffing for the very large churches, especially in the large cities. However, such staff must be (hired to equip rather than to perform ministry.)Churches with fewer than a hundred and fifty in attendance, unless newly planted and growing, will not usually be healthy in this model, but will usually become overly dependent upon the clergy. Financial considerations will also play a role in making it impossible to provide pastoral coverage for churches with fewer than one hundred and fifty in attendance. Yet finances must not be the deciding factor. Our motivation must be the health of the church.

n order for this model to work, the church must first of all create a mission mindset in the existing congregation or the newly planted church. People are not eager to receive training. If the pastor simply announces a training event, few people will actually show up for it, and most of them will be the wrong people. Instead, the church must first of all create a mission mindset in the church. Once a Great Commission consciousness has been established, people will desire training in order to facilitate the mission. People are not anxious to receive training just for the sake of being trained; they do want to be trained when they see how the training will enable the church to accomplish its mission. Thus a mission mindset in the church leads to training and results in both spiritual and numeric church growth.

However, a mission mindset is not developed overnight or simply by preaching a couple of sermons on mission.

There must be sermons, seminars, priority in the budget, priority in the board meetings, modeling, etc., occurring regularly in the church. When the people see that mission is the priority of the pastor and of the lay leadership, they will become a mission-minded church. It is out of this milieu that training will then be encouraged and people will willingly become a part of it and prioritize their time for training and actual ministry.

One further word on training. Most churches who attempt to train spend too much time in a classroom setting. Give people the basics they need in a short period of time and then immediately place them in a ministry context. They will not know everything they need to know, but they will then understand the right questions to ask at the next training session. Most trainings are so thorough that people actually become discouraged with attempting the ministry, but if they can first be placed in the ministry, they will learn much more rapidly and much more will be accomplished for God.

Model Two: The Small Rural Church

One of the greatest challenges to church planting and evangelism in the Adventist Church is the multitude of small rural churches that struggle just to survive at the beginning of the twenty-first century. Many of them are very small and have been declining for years. In several of them there are fewer than five worshipers each Sabbath. Most are grouped in districts of three or four other small churches. Several such districts would have a combined membership of fewer than one hundred. Yet a full-time pastor serves all four churches.

These kinds of churches really depend on the pastor to do everything. In some districts the pastor is expected to preach in each church at least twice a month and in some instances every Sabbath. Furthermore, the pastor is expected to have a weekly prayer meeting in each church, a monthly board meeting, etc. Traveling between the churches in the district conducting all these activities leaves little time for the pastor to evangelize and do what is needed to cause the small church to grow. Consequently, most small churches are either plateaued or declining. Also, in many cases these small churches are controlled by a matriarch or patriarch. The pastor needs to work through them in order to accomplish anything, but many times they are at odds with the pastor.

Rarely do such districts provide sufficient tithe to cover the cost to the conference in paying the pastor for the district. As a result, most such districts are heavily subsidized from the larger churches, which in turn prevents the conference from providing adequate pastoral coverage for them. This is also one of the reasons why it is so difficult for the conferences to provide new budgets for church planting in the major population centers. There are few funds available due to the heavy expense of staffing these small churches.

X (What can be done? Perhaps some of these small churches need to close) but that is not always easy or practical. We must find a way to care for these small groups without consuming so much of the limited resources of the church. We also need to find a way to provide them with the attention that they need to grow without having to depend on a paid staff to accomplish it.

X (The small church is a very valuable asset.) George Barna indicates that small churches will be viable in the twenty-first century because Generation X is very relationally oriented and wants small churches where relationships may be fostered. Having many small churches may enable the church to minister better to this oncoming generation. Therefore, we must not lose the small church, but we must learn how to make it more effective and cost efficient.

One possible solution is to utilize the pastoral arrangement that the third world has found so effective. In this model we would create large districts of fifteen to twenty churches, presided over by a district pastor. In this arrangement the pastor would act more like a mini conference president. He would facilitate the ministries of all the small churches in the district, but would not be the major performer of ministry in each church, as in the current arrangement. This size of district would actually be easier to pastor than three or four churches. In the smaller district, the membership still expects the pastor to do everything, but in the larger district, everyone would know that it would be impossible for the pastor to do everything. Therefore, the membership would assume more responsibility.

In this arrangement, the conference, under the direction of the district pastor, would need to appoint the head elder or lay pastor in each of the churches. Ideally, this would be an unpaid position, but some conferences might prefer to give a small stipend to the lay pastor to help with travel expenses. It would be imperative that this lay pastor or head elder be appointed rather than elected as normally, because of the need for the conference to hold the person accountable and be able to remove them if they should cease to be loyal to the church. One of the fears of lay leadership is that the conference would lose control and the leader would take the church off in the wrong direction or perhaps even lead it into a dissident group. Those are real concerns that need to be addressed. Appointment rather than election may be one way to solve the problem partially.

The district pastor would need to be in regular contact with these lay pastors or elders. Ideally, they would meet with the pastor once a month, perhaps on a Sunday. Three or four lay pastors/elders from churches in close proximity could come together for instruction, coaching, and training. This would enable the district leader to be in touch with what is happening in each church, provide counsel where needed, and provide any needed training. He would also need to be in daily contact with these lay pastors through e-mail and telephone.

The churches would benefit because the lay pastor or elder would give them more attention than they could receive from a pastor in a four-church district.

Conferences that have tried this approach of putting a lay

pastor over a church are reporting that the churches actually seem to thrive in this environment. Some that had fewer than five members have grown to twenty or more, whereas under the old arrangement they had been declining for years. Thus, this arrangement can actually benefit the existing church.

Who should pastor such a district? Probably the best pastors in the conference! Pastors who reveal leadership potential would thrive in this arrangement. They would be acting as mini conference presidents and would learn the skills necessary to facilitate leadership development. The pastor would occasionally preach at the churches, but primarily the lay pastor would provide the sermon, if the skill level were sufficient for that to happen. If not, the church could downlink a sermon from ACN every Sabbath, or have an old-fashioned testimony meeting in harmony with Ellen White's counsel that the members not expect a sermon every Sabbath.[26] The pastor in such a district, besides regularly training the people and consulting with them, would also be engaged in church planting. Under this model, new churches could continually be raised up in the district, making it possible to greatly accelerate the number of churches in the district without increasing the pastoral coverage. The pastor could periodically conduct evangelistic meetings or prophecy seminars in the district. Of course, laity would be doing this, too.

Money saved by combining districts could be used in several ways. For one, the conference could provide the pastoral coverage that large churches need to adequately evangelize their territory. However, the conferences would need to be careful to allocate these additional budgets based on the evangelistic activity of the church, and not just on the size of the existing membership. Second, budgets could be provided for church planting in the major metropolitan areas, where Adventism desperately needs hundreds of new churches. Church planting pastors could be sent into those areas to raise up many new churches. Third, the money saved could be used to create church planting teams, rather than solo pastors. This would bring the church into harmony with the counsel of Jesus to work two by two. All of this becomes possible when the resources are freed up from the excessive pastoral coverage currently occurring in the small churches.

This section has centered on the small rural church and suggested some alternatives. However, many small churches are also located in urban areas, many of which have been plateaued or declining for many years. There are not enough people (one hundred and fifty) to justify having a pastor. Perhaps these would need to be dealt with in the same way as the rural small church. All small urban churches in an area could be placed in one large district, or two metropolitan areas in a conference could be combined to create a large district. The pastor of this large district would serve in exactly the same way as would the pastor of a large district of small rural churches. The main difference would be the location of the churches. Since urban ministry differs from rural ministry, it would be wise to keep these two types of large districts separate and choose pastors for their ability to work best in the urban setting or the rural setting. Like their rural counterparts, the job of the urban pastor would be to counsel, train, evangelize, and church plant in the metropolitan areas.

There may be other solutions to the small church problem, but this can provide a springboard for discussion. If the Adventist Church is going to again become a church planting movement, it cannot afford to tie so many of its resources to the small churches. It must find a way to care for these X churches without consuming so many resources, and discover ways to make the small church grow and be more vibrant and healthy. The suggestions made here are meant to help foster this improvement by returning the small churches as quickly as possible to the early Adventist paradigm.

Churches cannot be forced into this model or they will resent it. They will need education into Ellen White's counsels regarding the work of the pastor and the need for nondependency. Once they are educated, they will need training to be able to function in the new paradigm. Only then can we move them to the large church districts that we have talked about here. As a mission mindset develops in these churches, many of them will request that care be provided in harmony with the counsel from Ellen White. In other words, this movement must arise from the people involved and not be legislated by the pastor or the conference. The conference and other levels can lend support for churches moving into the new paradigm; they can educate, but they must be careful not to legislate.

Model Three: The Cell Church

A third model of church that can fit the non-pastor-dependent paradigm is the cell church. This new kind of church is still in the testing period and only time will tell whether it truly becomes a viable model of church for Seventh-day Adventists. Yet, in theory at least, this model of church holds great promise for a non-pastor-dependent ministry.

The cell church is organized around small groups. It is different from a church that simply has small groups as one of many programs in the church. In the cell church, there are no other programs; all ministry emanates out of the cells. In the traditional church one can be a member of the church and not be part of a small group; in the cell church participation in the cell is more important than corporate worship, and one cannot be a member of the church unless participating in one of the cells.

All organization of the church centers in the cells.[27] A cell church does not have all the officers that traditional churches have—elders, deacons, personal ministries leaders, etc. In a cell church, the group leaders foster all kinds of ministries, which emanate from the cells. On Sabbath, the different groups in the church come together for joint worship, but that is secondary to the real life of the church, which transpires in the cell.

✗ (Cell churches place enormous energy into creating community.)Therefore, pastoral care functions in the cells, as fellow members of the cell provide care for each other. Cells are also evangelistic; they continually reach out, bring new people to faith, and nurture them within the safe environment of the cell. As a result, new cells are constantly forming in a cell church; ideally each cell fosters the birth of a new cell each year. As a result, this kind of church, once established, can realize exponential growth, as the church multiplies itself continually.

Cell churches can thrive anywhere, but they can realize their greatest potential in urban areas. One of the difficulties of planting churches in urban areas lies in the fact that property is so difficult to find and so expensive to buy. Since cell churches see property ownership as secondary, and since they mainly meet in the homes of believers as did the early Christians, purchasing a building is not necessary. They may rent a facility for the Sabbath worship of the groups, but generally they feel that putting millions of dollars into a building that will be used only once a week is unnecessary.

Cell churches do require a resident pastor, but the pastor is seen as the supervisor/trainer of all the groups. The main job of the pastor is to train group leaders, coach groups, foster the beginning of new cells, and evangelize. This role is in harmony with the principles enunciated by Ellen White. Here the pastor operates in a manner similar to the pastor of the twenty-church district, except that his twenty cells (churches) are all located in the same basic area. The pastor spends little time on pastoral care because the members within the cells care for one another. Only the difficult cases involve him.

There are several advantages to this model of ministry. First, it enables the pastor to handle large groups in a metropolitan area. Second, it provides the best possible pastoral care. Third, it enables the pastor to truly focus on church planting (starting new cells), for each new group started is, in essence, a new church. Fourth, it releases the energies of the church into accomplishing the mission of the church.

5. And finally, the church is built on the biblical and Ellen White counsels of nondependency.

Since this is such a different kind of church, it would be best to start such churches from scratch rather than try to transition an existing church into this model. An existing church is best transitioned into Model One. In starting cell churches, people need to be thoroughly immersed into the philosophy and practicality of doing cell church. They should read extensively in the literature and attend training events about starting cell churches; otherwise, they may start churches with small group appendages that are not truly cell churches. One of the key characteristics of these kinds of churches is the development of a strong discipleship track for new members in the cells. It is imperative in this model that the cell center on discipleship. Those who start cell churches without fully understanding the discipleship track will create what they may call cell churches, but which in reality are merely traditional churches with small groups as an appendage.

Conferences will need to be patient with this developing church. Generally it shows very slow growth in the first three years, because it is focused on developing its community base. However, after three years these churches virtually explode, provided they have developed the strong discipleship track mentioned above. Conferences will also need to be patient with these churches as they develop new forms of organization. For example, they do not have the traditional officers. If a conference insists that the cell church conform and elect the traditional officers, they will destroy it. If the cell movement is to grow, administration will need to allow for new forms and new names for roles that may function a little differently, yet still be thoroughly Adventist.

Model Four: The Lay Church

The fourth model of the non-pastor-dependent church is one that is totally run by laity, with no pastor. These churches are not even part of a multi-church district. They can be run like a traditional church or even a cell church. (The main 𝗫 difference is that there is no pastor, period!) In this sense, this church operates like most nineteenth-century Adventist churches. They care for themselves without a pastor and sustain their spiritual life and regular worship without the assistance of a pastor.

One of the best examples of this kind of church is the one that Rod and Donna Willey helped plan in the Peoria, Illinois, area. Rod is a full-time practicing dentist who started a church in his dental office. Eventually the church outgrew the dental office, and God led them to purchase a beautiful school in which to hold their services. The Richland Bridge Seventh-day Adventist Church is thoroughly Adventist. It operates like a traditional church only in the sense that it has various programs and ministries that emanate from the church. Thus, it is traditional in organization, and not cell based. However, it is nontraditional in the sense that all of the members are engaged in ministry. The church is not under the control of any one person; it is a church in the safe hands of laity. The church has never had a pastor and does not want one. It turns its tithe in to the Illinois Conference, as does any other church in the Conference. Last year (1998), the tithe amounted to around $85,000. Average attendance is between eighty-five and a hundred each Sabbath.

This model has tremendous potential for church planting in the Adventist church. Yet it is the most frightening to conference administration, and with good reason. If a pastor should attempt to lead a church into a dissident movement or be guilty of heresy, the conference could fire the pastor and save the church. However, in a lay church with an unpaid person in charge, the conference has no recourse.

Yet this model operated freely in early Adventism. It did, at times, have problems. Many times we read of James and Ellen White or other leaders visiting the churches to try to straighten out problems that developed, especially fanaticism. Yet even though there were problems with the model,

Ellen White and the others continued to advocate it. They did not seem to feel that the problems were insurmountable.

This model should be entered into only with lay people who are fiercely loyal to the Church and who will work in close harmony with the local conference administration. If a dialogue is created and church administration will stay in close touch with such churches, many successful churches may be established and many people won to the kingdom of God as a result.

Summation

In this chapter we have examined early Adventist church planting and discovered that the model advocated was clearly one of non-pastor-dependency. Early Adventists practiced this model to the extent that they advocated not having settled pastors over their churches. Instead, churches cared for themselves and maintained their regular worship without the aid of pastors, so that the pastors were free to evangelize and plant churches. Furthermore, when Adventism began to move away from this model in the first twenty years of the twentieth century, it was only the largest churches which had their own pastors, and these pastors were told not to hover over the church, but to be trainers and equippers.

As we enter the twenty-first century, we have proposed four models of nondependency that would be a modern adaptation of the principles of early Adventism. These models are: (1) the traditional church with a pastor who is seen primarily as a trainer/equipper rather than primary caregiver, (2) the small church district with lay pastors/elders over the local church and a pastor over fifteen to twenty such churches, (3) the cell church, where the church is organized around the groups and the pastor primarily fosters new groups and coaches existing groups, while at the same time preaching to all the groups each Sabbath, and (4) the lay church, which has no pastor but is run by laity in close counsel with the local conference, and who are absolutely loyal to the church in doctrine and to the local conference administration.

(All of these models can help the Seventh-day Adventist Church in North America begin to focus on church planting as a major activity.) It can also help the church free its resources to be more harvest-centered. Adventist eschatology has always foreseen a time when persecution will occur and members will have to exist without the benefit of clergy. These models not only will help the church grow now, but will help members prepare for the final time of trouble when the church will have to exist on its own. Since this way of doing church is so ingrained in Adventist history and eschatology, it is imperative that present-day Adventism seek to revive this model of non-pastor-dependent churches by planting many new churches in these models.

Notes:

1. These were what early Adventist literature refers to as the First-day Adventists.

2. Dale, *To Dream Again*, 16-18.

3. Loughborough, *The Church: Its Organization*, 127.

4. Ibid.

5. Ibid., 103.

6. James White, *Review and Herald*, April 15, 1862. Vol. XIX, No. 20, 156.

7. Ibid.

8. These figures are based on surveys of conferences in preparation for the *Seeds* convention in July of 1998.

9. Interview with G. B. Starr, reported in the Wabash, Indiana, *Plain Dealer*, October 1, 1886, 5.

10. *Seventh-day Baptist Sabbath Recorder*, December 28, 1908 reported in *Review and Herald* of January 14, 1909.

11. A. G. Daniells, Ministerial Institute Address, Los Angeles, California, March 1912.

12. Ellen G. White, *Christian Service* (Takoma Park, Washington, DC: General Conference of Seventh-day Adventists, 1947), 61.

13. Ellen G. White, *Review and Herald*, May 7, 1889.

14. For a discussion of the early Adventist worship service, see the author's book, *The Revolutionized Church of the 21st Century* (Fallbrook, Calif.: Hart Research Center, 1997).

15. Ellen G. White, Loma Linda Messages, 179, 180.

16. Ellen G. White, "The Work in Greater New York," *Atlantic Union Gleaner*, January 8, 1902.

17. Ellen G. White, *Review and Herald*, October 27, 1910.

18. Ellen G. White, *Acts of the Apostles* (Mountain View, Calif.: Pacific Press, 1911), 105; idem., *Fundamentals of Christian Education*, 267.

19. Ellen G. White, *Testimonies*, vol. 7, 18; idem., *Evangelism*, 113; idem., *Testimonies*, vol. 7, 19; Ibid., 18, 19.

20. H.M.S. Richards, *Feed My Sheep* (Washington, D.C.: Review and Herald, 1958), 156.

21. See Loren B. Mead, *The Once and Future Church* (New York: The Alban Institute, 1994), for a discussion of the historical development of the Middle Ages model. Also see the work by this author: *An Understanding of Clergy Role Based on Biblical and Adventist Historical Roots* (Berrien Springs, Mich.: NADEI, 1994).

22. Ellen G. White, *Evangelism*, 381.

23. GC Bulletin, April 21, 1901, Extra No. 16, 27.

24. G.C. Bulletin, April 21, 1901.

25. For a discussion of this role as outlined in Ephesians 4, see the author's book *Revolution in the Church* (Fallbrook, Calif.: Hart Research Center, 1993). The primary chapters would be those on the role of the laity and the work of the pastor.

26. Adventist Communication Network (ACN) provides a weekly sermon by satellite.

27. "Cell" refers to a group of no more than fifteen people that meets together regularly.

4

Ellen White and Church Planting

In the previous chapter we explored early Adventist church planting and discovered that it was the primary mission objective of the church. Adventism was primarily a church planting movement. Ellen White was a vital part of that strategy. She understood church planting to be the primary role of the pastor. She also made other specific references to church planting. We will examine these references in this short chapter.

Her most inclusive statement on church planting is that: "Upon all who believe, God has placed the burden of raising up churches."[1] Church planting is not an option for any Seventh-day Adventist. While not everyone is going to become a church planter, every believer is to support the church planting endeavor and carry the burden for its accomplishment. Our entire membership must become passionate about church planting. When Dr. Robert Logan, Conservative Baptist church planting consultant, spoke at the first Seeds Conference in 1996, he opened his remarks by asking how many were believers. When all raised their hands, he then quoted to us the above statement from Ellen White. Sometimes it takes someone from outside our church to quote Ellen White to us before we listen to the tremendous counsel that she has given for the church.

Throughout her ministry Ellen White counseled the church to develop a church planting strategy that would place Adventism in every city and village. Listen to her oft-repeated counsel:

> New churches must be established, new congregations organized. At this time there should be representatives in every city and in the remote parts of the earth.
>
> In all countries and cities the gospel is to be proclaimed. . . . Churches are to be organized and plans laid for work to be done by the members of the newly organized churches.
>
> Place after place is to be visited, church after church is to be raised up.[2]

Ellen White constantly emphasized the need for extended and continual church planting. She envisioned Adventism belting the globe, with churches being established in just about every corner of planet Earth. There is an interesting twist in the middle statement above. Not only were churches to be raised up, but as soon as they were raised up, the members of those new churches were to be put to work. Here again is Ellen White's unqualified endorsement of the new members immediately being educated, trained for ministry, and then deployed. There were to be no idlers in Adventist churches; all members were to be workers.

Finances are always a major concern when the subject of church planting arises. And rightly so. We must plant churches, but we must also be financially solvent. The early Adventist church faced these same problems. At times there must have been those who suggested that the church not plant so rapidly, but instead spend more time with the established churches. It is in this setting that Ellen White seems

to be answering the critics of church planting who use finances as an excuse not to plant more churches:

> The establishment of churches, the erection of
> meeting-houses and school-buildings, was ex-
> tended from city to city, and the tithe was increas-
> ing to carry forward the work. Plants were made
> not only in one place, but in many places, and the
> Lord was working to increase His forces.

> Let not the work of establishing memorials for
> God in many places be made difficult and burden-
> some because the necessary means is withheld.[3]

Evidently there were those who were making church planting difficult in her day by holding back some of the money
that should have been going into church planting and using
it for other things. Such attempts to hinder the church planting movement of the Adventist church met sharp rebuke from
the prophet of the Lord. Absolutely nothing was to hinder
the church from making church planting a major priority of
the church. Therefore she reassures the brethren that if they
will continue to plant churches, new tithe will be produced
to support the expanding work. In Ellen White's view, money
was never the problem; it was always a question of priorities. Church planting was to be the top priority for a mission-driven church.

Ellen White's vision for church planting was extensive. No
place was too large or too small for an Adventist church to
be created. Some of these statements are visions of what
God showed her would happen when God's people obeyed
Him and made church planting a top priority:

> The people who bear His sign are to establish
> churches and institutions as memorials to Him

> God's workers are to plant the standards of truth
> in every place to which they can gain access. Me-
> morials for Him are to be raised in America and in
> foreign countries.

> I saw jets of light shining from cities and villages, and from high places and the low places of the earth. God's word was obeyed, and as a result there were memorials for Him in every city and village. His truth was proclaimed throughout the world.
>
> In every city where the truth is proclaimed, churches are to be raised up. In some large cities there must be churches in various parts of the city.[4]

In vision Ellen White saw that the Adventist church would be faithful; it would move out into all the world and plant churches everywhere. She identifies these churches as memorials for God and then states that as a result of obeying God's word to plant churches, Adventist churches were planted in *every* city and village on the planet. Such a statement is mind-boggling because it does not state every city, but every city and village. And this is not counsel—it is a *vision* of what she saw happening as a result of Adventists obeying God about planting churches.

To plant an Adventist church in every city and village on the planet is impossible with our present methods. We could never afford to place a congregation in every village with a building and a hired pastor. Obviously, Ellen White is not talking about traditional church planting; she is suggesting planting churches in the paradigm of early Adventism. Only as we move back to this paradigm does it become possible to fulfill the vision.

However, the greatest current need for church planting is in the major metropolitan areas of North America. Adventism is grossly under-represented in these major population belts. Here is fertile territory for immediate and large church planting. In the last statement quoted above, Ellen White clarifies the need for planting a multitude of new churches in the major urban areas of North America and the world.

In the final fifteen years of her life, Ellen White constantly urged the church toward an aggressive plan of city evangelism. She realized that Adventism had primarily been a rural movement throughout the nineteenth century. It had grown as the nation moved westward. But beginning in 1900, North America began an urban migration that has continued for the entire century. With prophetic insight, Ellen White urged the church to move with the people flow and begin to plant churches aggressively in the cities that were beginning to mushroom in population.

It took her more than ten years to get the attention of the brethren. Her parting passion for the Adventist church in North America was for city evangelism. Adventism has still failed to heed her message, and therefore at the beginning of the twenty-first century, the Adventist church continues to be primarily a rural church, especially in its Anglo membership. In fact, if all non-Anglo groups were eliminated from the cities, the Adventist presence in most cities would be nonexistent. Yet in most major cities, the majority of the population is Anglo. Here is a urgent need for aggressive church planting.

Ellen White finally got the attention of A. G. Daniells in 1910 when he decided to pay her a visit in California. Ellen White had been urging him for some time to support city evangelism, but he had failed to give it the needed attention. When Daniells went to Elmshaven to see the prophetess, she refused to see him until he began to follow the counsel which he had already been given. Daniells declared it to be the most humiliating experience of his life, but it got his attention, and he went back and recommitted the Church to city evangelism. However, a lot of ground had been lost in the ten years it had taken to get his attention, and it was six more years before the plan could really be put into action. The result has been that Adventists really have never penetrated the cities.

While the non-pastor-dependency model with churches in large districts of fifteen to twenty churches enables us to plant churches in all the small places, it also frees up salaries to hire church planters to go into our cities and plant a multitude of churches in these great, neglected urban centers.

Are the people in the cities more important than the people in rural areas? Of course not. It is just that there are more people in the urban areas. It makes good stewardship sense to invest the Church's limited resources where the greatest number of people can be reached.

There were several reasons why Ellen White felt that church planting should be one of the top priorities of the Adventist church. First, it would bring spiritual renewal to the members of large churches. If large churches would simply plant a church, they would be in much better spiritual health. It was not God's plan for large groups of people to gather in one place and then fail to reach out and plant new churches. This failure to minister would result in weak churches with sick members:

> Many of the members of our large churches are doing comparatively nothing. They might accomplish a good work if, instead of crowding together, they would scatter into places that have not yet been entered by the truth. Trees that are planted too thickly do not flourish. They are transplanted by the gardener, that they may have room to grow and not become dwarfed and sickly. The same rule would work well for our large churches. Many of the members are dying spiritually for want of this very work. They are becoming sickly and inefficient.[5]

Second, church planting as a priority for Adventism would bring church renewal. This need is clearly mentioned in the above quotation. Planting new churches will renew sickly, dying churches. There is nothing more calculated to bring life to churches than birthing a new baby church. Just as elderly people light up around the presence of babies, so do elderly churches.

Third, church planting enables the church to reach every possible soul with the message of salvation. If everyone was to be reached with the three angels' messages, then churches had to be planted everywhere. This mission concern is found throughout Ellen White's constant pleas for aggressive church planting.

Fourth, Ellen White desired pastors to plant churches because it would cause them to value souls. When they saw what it takes to reach a soul, they would be more careful what they did to souls when they ministered in existing churches. The amazing thing is that Ellen White made this statement when the church did not have settled pastors.

> Frequently the churches are in advance of the ministers who labor among them, and would be in a more prosperous condition if those ministers would keep out of their way and give them an opportunity to work. . . . If they would leave the churches, go out into the new fields, and labor to raise up churches, they would understand their ability and what it costs to bring souls out to take their position upon the truth.[6]

Fifth, church planting cultivates a missionary spirit and eradicates selfishness. Ellen White considered it sinful and selfish for churches to try to keep large congregations together rather than to constantly be starting new churches. If the people of God were to represent Him to the world, and selfishness is the root of sins, then selfishness had to be eradicated from the church. Ellen White felt that church planting was one way that helped a church eliminate selfishness from its corporate life:

> The seeds of truth are to be sown in uncultivated centers. . . . It will cultivate a missionary spirit to work in new localities. Selfishness in respect to keeping large companies together is not the Lord's plan. Enter every new place possible and begin the work of educating in vicinities that have not heard the truth.[7]

Sixth, church planting is the clear mission mandate of Christ. It will enable the church to reach the world with the message of God's love. The only way for the church to continually expand into new areas is to engage in aggressive church planting.

> This gospel missionary work is to keep reaching out and annexing new territory, enlarging the cultivated portions of the vineyards. The circle is to extend until it belts the world. From town to town, from city to city, from country to country, the warning message is to be proclaimed, not with outward display, but in the power of the Spirit, by men of faith.[8]

In this rapid survey of Ellen White's view of church planting, we must not neglect a major concern which echos the message of the previous chapter. Pastors were simply spending too much time caring for existing congregations when God had called them to go forth to the neglected areas of God's vineyard and bring forth abundant fruit for God's harvest.

> The Lord's great vineyard demands from men that which it has not yet received–earnest, persevering labor for souls. The ministry is becoming weak and feeble, and under their tame service the churches also are becoming weak. The ministers of our conferences have very little to show in the conversion of souls as a result of their labors. These things are depriving God of the glory which belongs to Him. The truth is not carried into the barren places of the earth. God calls for workers who will be producers. There is a world to be warned. Why are the ministers who should be laboring in special service earnestly to open new fields and rise up new churches, hovering over the churches which have already received great light and many advantages which they do not appreciate.[9]

> The greatest cause of our spiritual feebleness as a people, is the lack of real faith in Spiritual Gifts. If they all received this kind of testimony in full faith, they would put from them those things which

displease God, and would everywhere stand in union and in strength. And three-fourths of the ministerial labor now expended to help the churches could then be spared to the work of raising up churches in new fields.[10]

Ellen White is quite emphatic. Church planting is the crying need of the Adventist church. It must develop a harvest mentality, where the needs of the lost consume us with great passion to reach them. That is what created this deep passion in the heart of Ellen White for church planting. People in ministry, in harmony with their spiritual gifts, create freedom from pastoral dependency in existing churches. The result is the pastors are free to raise up new churches.

Even A. G. Daniells caught the church planting vision of Ellen White: "I reckon it would do every conference president good to occasionally drop out of office and spend a year raising up churches."[11] Such thoughts seem foreign to the church today, but they were normal thoughts in a church that was a church planting movement.

Ellen White was also concerned that church planters be multiplied. Rather than simply using the same people for new church after new church, she felt that new churches would supply new people for the church planting process. In this way church planting would occur naturally and spontaneously.

> As churches are established, it should be set before them that it is even from among them that men must be taken to carry the truth to others, and raise up new churches, therefore they must all work, and cultivate to the utmost the talents that God has given them, and be training their minds to engage in the service of their Master.[12]

This rapid survey of Ellen White's understanding of church planting reveals that she considered it to be the primary function of the Adventist church. All other church activities were to take a back seat to the aggressive church planting initiative that she fostered. Her concern was for the harvest and that the harvest be reached. Therefore, since the Adventist church was a church in mission, church planting must consume the bulk of the resources of the church. The time, talent, and treasure of the church should be expended on the harvest, if the church was to be a Great Commission church. Ellen White was also concerned for other aspects of Adventism, but church planting was her unabated passion throughout her nearly ninety years. If the prophet God sent had such a passion for church planting, how dare the present-day church be any less passionate about planting churches to reach the great harvest that God desires to reap.

Notes:

1. Ellen G.White, *Medical Ministry* (Mountain View, Ca: Pacific Press, 1963), 315.

2. Ellen G.White, *Testimonies*, vol. 6, 24; *Evangelism*, 19; *Testimonies*, vol. 7, 20.

3. Ellen G.White, *Gospel Workers*, 435; *Testimonies*, vol. 9, 132, 133.

4. Ellen G. White, *Testimonies*, vol. 7, 105; *Selected Messages*, vol. 1 (Washington, D.C.: Review and Herald, 1958), 112; *Testimonies*, vol. 9, 28, 29; *Medical Ministry*, 309.

5. Ellen G.White, *Testimonies*, vol. 8, 244.

6. Ellen G.White, *Testimonies*, vol. 2, 340.

7. Ellen G.White, *Evangelism*, 47.

8. Ibid., 19.

9. Ellen G.White, *Manuscript Releases*, Vol. 13, 208.

10. Ellen G.White, *Review and Herald*, January 14, 1868.

11. Arthur White, *Ellen G. White Biography*, vol. 6 (Washington, DC: Review and Herald, 1984), 451.

12. Ellen G.White, *Christian Service*, 61.

5

Why Plant a Church Today?

Church planting was the primary evangelistic activity of the earliest Christians, as well as of the fledgling Adventist community. Is it still an option today for effectively evangelizing lost communities? In this chapter we wish to explore the rationale for planting churches at the beginning of the twenty-first century.

Church growth guru Peter Wagner has declared: "The single most effective evangelistic methodology under heaven is planting new churches."[1] This church growth expert recognizes that Ellen White's priority of church planting is still the most effective means of evangelization today. In fact, every growing denomination has an effective church planting strategy.

> Every denomination reporting an increase in membership reports an increase in the number of congregations. Every denomination reporting an increase in the total number of congregations reports an increase in members. Every denomination reporting a decrease in membership reports a decrease in congregations. Every denomination re-

porting a decrease in congregations reports a decrease in members. . . . The first step in developing a denominational strategy for church growth should be to organize new congregations.[2]

Ellen White's counsel to the Church over one hundred years ago is still remarkably applicable to the present situation. Church planting is a necessary ingredient for any denomination that is serious about fulfilling the gospel commission. Interestingly, an examination of Adventist conferences by the author noted that generally those conferences that planted more churches over a thirty year period experience significantly higher growth than those conferences who did not plant many new churches. While there are many factors at work in any growth formula, it appears that church planting is a necessary ingredient.

There are several reasons why new churches should be planted today. First is the strong biblical and Ellen White support for church planting. The New Testament church and the early Adventist church both grew because they made church planting a top priority. That alone should motivate us to prioritize church planting.

Second, church planting is the most efficient method of evangelism, as Peter Wagner has noted. Money invested in church planting will result in a greater harvest than funds invested in any other method of evangelism. New churches actually reach more people than mature churches. In fact, the older a congregation becomes, the less efficient it becomes in reaching the harvest. One study revealed that younger churches required only six members to baptize one convert, whereas older churches required twenty-five members to baptize one new convert.[3] Research in the Adventist church confirms Wagner's findings:

> Churches where most members have been in the church for twenty or more years are not growing. Growing churches have a greater proportion of their membership made up of recent converts. . . . New converts are the best potential soul-winners

because they still have many contacts with non-church members. . . . And often the new convert in his first love will be more active in telling his friends what the Lord has done for him.[4]

Third, church planting will stimulate growth in an older church. A church that is on a plateau or even in decline can actually be stimulated back into a growth cycle by starting a new church. Many times mature congregations grow complacent, especially if they are comfortably full. The start of a new church with some of its members leaving creates a void in the existing church that in turn stimulates them into action. The status quo is no longer viable. As a result, the mother church returns to a growth cycle.

This is seen especially in urban areas where there have been only one or two Adventist churches. These churches have assumed that anyone who was an Adventist would join their church, since there were no other options. However, let a new church start in the area, and suddenly there are options for people. In order to stay competitive, the old church needs to spruce up its program and avoid complacency. This may not be the best reason for planting, but it is one of the consequences of starting a church in an area where there is an existing church.

Fourth, new churches will require new leaders for both the mother church and the new church. The need for more people to be involved in leadership means that an increased number of members will become active in the church. Having a greater percentage of laity involved results in a healthier church. Many times a new church plant will attract some of the best people in the mother church. Church planting is on the cutting edge of ministry, and people who want to be where there is action are attracted to the new plant. Suddenly the mother church finds itself losing its best leadership. Other potential leaders, who had not been utilized because of the dominance of these leaders, now surface in the mother church and replace them. More available leadership positions mean that more people will become involved in the church and the ultimate result is spiritual growth for both the original church and the newly planted church.

Many times people in existing churches are inactive simply because there is a wealth of talent available in the church. Sometimes some of them even cease to be regular in church attendance. In one new church that God helped us to raise up, a woman transferred from an existing area Adventist church. I discovered that she was an inactive member of that church, only attending once a quarter. Joining the new church, she started attending every Sabbath, got involved in the life of the church, was elected into a leadership position, became a soul winner and eventually saw her son and husband baptized. All of this probably would never have happened without the new church plant that provided her a place to get involved.

The fifth reason for planting churches today is selfish, but is also very real. The survival of the denomination is at stake. One only has to ask how many churches are still here that existed a hundred years ago to know that if new churches had not been planted, very few Adventist churches would now exist. As someone has suggested, we are only one generation away from the extinction of Christianity. We will explore this reason later in the chapter when we discuss the life cycle of churches.

Sixth, planting new churches enables us to reach the present generation. This is a more important reason today than in previous generations. The emergence of the Boomers and Generation X has resulted in more significant generational differences than previously. Any church that ignores these differences will not reach significant numbers of these generations.

Churches have a tendency to take on the characteristics of the generation that formed it. For example, a church birthed in the 1930s during the great depression that gripped North America took on the characteristics of that generation. Those characteristics included, among other things, frugality and a reluctance to buy anything on credit. In contrast, the present generation sees nothing wrong with incurring debt in order to get what you need immediately. Without making a judgment call on either generation, churches that have the characteristic of frugality and no debt have a difficult time relating to those who believe that realistic debt is one way to advance the work of the church more quickly.

As time continues, those who join a church that was started in the 1930s are usually those who feel pretty much the same as did the original founders. Thus, even though most of the founders have left or died, the church still carries those basic qualities advocated by the founders. The problem for this church is that fewer and fewer people relate to those qualities, thus fewer people join this church, and ultimately most such churches die.

A new church will take on the characteristics of the present generation. While it, too, may become obsolete in thirty years, it is the only hope of reaching new generations. Now, it needs to be recognized that all churches will appeal to some people of each generation, but if the church wishes to reach significant numbers of the present generation, it is absolutely necessary to plant churches today that specifically target the present generations. As the Oldsmobile commercial stated: "This is not your father's Oldsmobile."

Seventh, new churches allow the denomination to reach a more diversified group of people. Having more churches provides more options for people. Adventists today will drive past three or four churches to attend the one they relate to. The day of the neighborhood church is gone, especially in metropolitan areas. People choose a church today not on the basis of geography, but on how it relates to them. Different churches have different characteristics. Adventist churches are not identical. In one major metropolitan area you may find an Adventist church that ministers primarily to family, one that caters to singles, one that provides a home for divorced people, and another that focuses on younger people. Even within the theological spectrum of Adventism some churches cater to a more conservative Adventist lifestyle, some are more middle of the road, and others consider themselves progressive. All may be vibrant Adventist churches, but having so many choices enables the church to reach more people. Another benefit of multiple churches is that they provide a place where people who disagree with something in one church can find a community where they can still be an Adventist. When there is only one choice, many of these people drop out, but multiple churches provide a better chance for these people to discover a church where they fit.

Eighth, having more churches in an area helps the community to be more aware of the Adventist presence. An Adventist church in a city of 300,000, even if it is a large church, is hardly noticed, but ten Adventist churches in that same city will be more visible, even if the individual churches are smaller. The more frequently the name Seventh-day Adventist appears, the more aware people become of the church. As a result, more people are won to Christ and to the church. Two churches will simply win more people to Christ than one would.

An experiment was done in two churches. In one church, every group of twelve or more people was divided into two groups, while in the other church, every group of fewer than twelve were combined with another group. After six months, the groups that had combined had reduced their size to the original size of one of the combined groups; whereas in the church that had divided the groups, all the groups had grown to the size of the original group. Combining churches results in loss of membership, but starting new churches results in increased attendance in the church.

Ninth, the mobility of society today demands that new churches constantly be planted in areas to which people are moving. There may be sections of a town that were sparsely populated ten years ago but now are booming communities. A church needs to be planting in these areas. What was a wheat field ten years ago is now an unentered area for the Adventist church, and must be infiltrated with the gospel.

The places in which the truth has never been proclaimed are the best places in which to work. The truth is to take possession of the will of those who have never heard it.[5]

There has been a failure on the part of all denominations to keep pace with the accelerating population of North America. In 1900 there were 27 churches for every 10,000 Americans. In 1985 there were only 12 churches for every 10,000 Americans. In 1900 there was one church for every 370 people. By 1985 there was only one church for every 833 people. Today there are approximately 350,000 churches of all denominations in America, and 4,700 of them are Seventh-day Adventist. Based on the declining ratio of churches to population, Win Arn, church growth consultant, suggested that we could double the number of churches in America and still not be over-churching America.

Tenth, new churches need to be organized to reach the multitude of ethnic populations that exist in North America. The main reason for Adventist growth in the last several years is that Adventists have been seriously planting churches in ethnic populations. As a result, Adventist penetration into most major ethnic groups is better than would be expected for a denomination of our size.

We must not fail to continue to plant churches in all these ethnic groups because they are the future. In fact, it is projected that by the year 2050, ethnic groups in the United States will surpass the traditional Anglo population. Probably more than 50 percent of North American membership in Adventism will be ethnic within the first decade of the twenty-first century.

To reach these ethnic groups will require that we continually plant first-generation ethnic churches. When people first immigrate, they are most open to the gospel and to Adventism. Therefore, we must not neglect the continuous planting of ethnic churches, for older ethnic churches will soon cease to reach the incoming populations.

Objections to Church Planting

In spite of all the commands to plant churches, many still offer objections to church planting today. While some of these objections are just excuses, others are real, and we need to try to work through them. In this section we wish to look briefly at some of the major objections offered against church planting.

1. **It will harm the mother church**. "If we plant a new church, we will lose some of our major supporters, our finances will drop, and we won't have enough people left to staff the church." This is probably one of the most common excuses used for not planting churches. However, there is no credible evidence that church planting harms the mother church when done properly. All the evidence suggests that it actually has a positive effect upon the mother church.

It is true that the mother church usually experiences a drop in attendance and a drop in financial support for about six months at the time of the church plant. After that the mother church usually experiences an increase in both attendance and finances. God seems to bless church planting so that starting a new church is rarely a solution for an overcrowded situation. More room results in increased attendance, and the church continues to be overcrowded. But, in addition, there is the daughter church, so the harvest is greatly increased.

There have been a few instances where a church plant has hurt the mother church. Usually in such instances the mother church had opposed the new plant, but still it happened. God has a hard time blessing a church with a poor attitude. At other times the parent church has been hurt because too many people were taken from the mother church for the new plant. The new church should never take more than 15 percent of the attendance of the existing church or it is apt to harm the mother church. Also a mother church needs some time to recover between plants. Planting too many churches too rapidly could harm the mother church. Remember, the church needs at least six months to recover and then a few months to be able to regain some resources before the next plant begins. Yet at the same time a church will not want to wait too long between plants or it will also miss the blessing.

2. It costs too much money to start a new church. The traditional method for starting churches *has* been expensive, yet even so it is the most cost effective means of evangelism in terms of dollars spent. Public evangelism in the North America Division averages between $1,000 and $2,000 per convert, whereas a new church plant cost only $60 for each individual. This is not to negate public evangelism. Many church plants begin out of evangelistic meetings, and this is a very effective way of beginning new congregations. The point is that church planting is not any more expensive, and may even be less expensive, than more traditional evangelistic methodologies.

Church planting costs vary greatly by denominations. Presbyterians, for example, reveal that it costs them $500,000 for each new plant. Included in the start-up costs are the building and the pastor's salary for the first year. In contrast, the Assemblies of God indicate that it costs them only $2,500 for each new church. The new pastor simply gets a job in the community, and they rent a church. As a result, the Assemblies of God plant a lot more churches than do the Presbyterians. Adventists must learn to plant churches inexpensively.

The best church plants actually are those that are not subsidized for too long. To give a church a continuing subsidy in the long run develops a "welfare mentality" in the mind of the new church, with a dependency on the conference or the mother church that is not healthy. Remember, the resources are in the harvest. We must not be afraid to teach new converts stewardship and tithing. As soon as people start contributing to the church and taking ownership of the church, they will feel that it is their church. In the first few years, it is best if the new church puts all its resources into people rather than bricks and mortar. New churches should not build too soon. In fact, most churches plateau after they build, because all their money and time now is going into keeping up the building and paying off the mortgage, whereas before it was going into the harvest and reaching people. Buildings may be needed at a certain time, but most new churches build too soon.

3. **A church plant would mean the loss of fellowship with many brothers and sisters.** Of course, this is true. Many of the people that we have grown close to in Christian fellowship may move out and join the new church, and we will lose their fellowship in the mother church. Yet this is one of the prices we pay for extending the kingdom of God. The same people who complain about losing people to a new church never complain when these same people leave because of a job transfer. Why can we accept their leaving for personal reasons, but not to advance the cause of God?

One of the hardest things for Christians to accept is the priority of Jesus. With Jesus, the love of God for the lost is a higher priority than the care of existing Christians (parable of the lost sheep). This obviously does not mean that caring for existing Christians needs to be low priority, but the church must remember that reaching the lost is the top priority. Nothing can be allowed to usurp mission as the church's primary function. Churches need to begin looking at planting new churches not as competitive, but as complimentary. Two churches will simply reach more of the harvest than one church. There is no competition for the harvest—the only competition is for existing saints. That is the reason that we need to plant harvest-driven churches, and not plant churches merely to redistribute the saints. The motivation for starting churches clearly must be the harvest, and for that there is no competition.

4. **We already have too many churches; we simply need to fill up the ones we already have.** If this is so, why hasn't Jesus come? One has to have blinders on to think that we have enough churches for the harvest that God wants to give us. If the existing churches need to be filled up, why isn't that happening? The fact that a church has been in pla-

teau or decline for years is evidence enough that this church is never going to reach the harvest. It will take in replacement members, but it has become ineffective in reaching much of the harvest.

The tragedy is that many lost people are turned off by our existing churches. Not that they are doing things wrong. They do many things right for the people they reach, but the diversification of the harvest is so great today that many different kinds of churches need to be planted to reach the diverseness of the harvest. We can hope that many existing churches will turn around, but the sad reality that the denomination must face is that many of these churches never will change. If we are serious about reaching the harvest in that area, we will need to plant a new church that will reach that group of people. As Peter Wagner declared, "It is easier to have babies than to raise the dead. And it is more fun."[6]

Adventists are well represented in most rural areas. Yet Adventist churches are greatly under-represented in the major metropolitan areas of North America. What many administrators fear about church planting is that it will result in a multitude of small rural churches and that trying to supply pastors to all of them will further drain the system. However, that need not happen if the early Adventist model of non-pastor-dependency is used. The greatest need for Adventist church planting is in the cities. The church needs to solve the problem of supplying pastors for these small rural churches, which are draining the resources, so that money can be freed up to enter the cities and reach the masses. Adventism simply does not have enough churches in the major urban centers. This must become the target of serious church planting.

The Life Cycle of Churches

Most churches go through a life cycle of seventy to eighty years. During that time the church goes through phases of birth, growth, plateau, decline, and death. The life cycle of a church is very similar to the life cycle of most humans. Robert Dale has suggested that churches go through the following stages in the course of their life cycle: dream, beliefs, goals, structure, ministry, nostalgia, questions, polarization, and disintegration.[7]

In Dale's analysis there are four stages on the upside of the life cycle and four stages on the downside of the life cycle, with ministry being at the height or top of the cycle. A church begins with a dream on the part of those who form the church. They vision together to create a church that God can use. As time progresses, they begin putting their beliefs together, as to what they feel about their church and what they believe God is calling that church to do. Once the dream and belief are in place, the church then creates goals to help it accomplish its dream and beliefs. Yet in order to accomplish those goals, the church needs structure. So structure is created to support the goals. Structure is not the pilot that drives the church—the dream drives the church and structure is subservient to the dream. The result is ministry performance and the accomplishment of many wonderful acts for God.

However, on the downside of the life cycle the reverse begins to happen. After a plateau develops, many in the church begin to look back on the olden days, as nostalgia sets in. Remarks such as "Remember when Pastor Jones was here?" seem to be heard more often. As nostalgia continues, it moves into questioning, as people begin to question what has gone wrong. Why is the church no longer as effective as it was in the past? Differing opinions are offered, many of which have nothing to do with reality.

As a result of questions, the church ultimately moves into polarization. The members divide into warring camps and begin fighting with each other, each blaming something different for what has gone wrong. The energy of the church now gets channeled into fighting battles within rather than the real battle for souls. Ultimately, the church falls apart and dies.

That is the natural life cycle of churches. Obviously, no church wants this to happen, but this is the road most travel. When a church finds itself on the downside of its life cycle, there are some things it can do. Most churches in this stage begin to play with the structure of the church, thinking that will solve their problem. In actuality the structure was developed to support the dream, but the church has lost sight of the dream. Therefore, any church on the downside of its life cycle must go back and rebirth the dream, working again through the upside of the life cycle and recreating structure only in response to the new dream that it has envisioned.

The reality is that 90 percent of all churches will plateau by the time of their fifteenth birthday. Many will plateau long before that time. Some churches can ride that plateau for thirty, forty, or fifty years, depending on their location and ministry, but inevitably they will move into decline. All churches would like to think that they are the exception, but life cycles are hard to break, and it is rare to find an exception to the life cycle rule.

Why discuss life cycles in a chapter on the need to plant new churches? For this reason: If 90 percent of the churches plateau by their fifteenth birthday, and since 90 percent of the churches in the North American Division are over fifteen years old, then 80 percent to 90 percent of all churches in North America are plateaued or declining. That explains why it is so difficult for major growth to occur in North America.

Most growth occurs in the newly planted churches, which comprise only 10 percent to 20 percent of the membership. Increasing the number of new churches would therefore greatly accelerate the growth of the North American Division. Failure to move into a church planting mission means a continuation of plateau for North America, and eventual decline. The future of the Adventist Church in North America is at stake. As our churches age, they will become less and less effective in reaching the harvest. The ultimate end is decline, unless the denomination aggressively plants new churches.

Take a look at older churches. They can hold one evangelistic meeting after another, but the attendance remains the same. They don't lose the new members; the new members simply replace those lost through attrition. Metropolitan areas that rely only on their existing membership to evangelize their communities usually will have the same attendance ten years later, but if they add a church, they will discover that the attendance in the area has increased by the number of people meeting in the new congregation.

An examination of the life cycle provides proof that the Church needs to become serious about church planting. The aging churches of the North American Division will continue to become less and less effective as we move into the twenty-first century. This will not be deliberate—it is the inevitable consequence of growing old. Old first church that used to be the plum church in the Conference is now becoming a declining church and is no longer looked at as one of the ideal places to pastor in Adventism. It has seen its day. If new churches do not arise to take the place of the great Adventist churches of the 1970s, Adventism will die. This must not happen. Church planting is critical to the survival of Adventism in the land of its birth.

Notes:

1. C. Peter Wagner, *Church Planting for a Greater Harvest* (Ventura, CA: Regal Books, 1990), 11.

2. Lyle Schaller, "Commentary: What Are the Alternatives?" *Understanding Church Growth and Decline*, Dear R. Hoge and David A. Roozen, eds. (New York: Pilgrim, 1979), 351, 352.

3. C. Peter Wagner, *Greater Harvest*, 33.

4. Roger Dudley, *Ministry*, July 1981, 6.

5. E. G. White, Letter 106, 1903.

6. Statement made by Peter Wagner during a church planting seminar attended by the author.

7. For a discussion of this life cycle track, see Robert Dale, *To Dream Again.*

6

Who Should Plant a Church?

Ellen White has made it clear to Seventh-day Adventists that "upon all who believe, God has placed the burden of raising up churches."[1] Yet she did not declare that all who believe should *plant* churches. While everyone is to share the burden of raising up new churches, church planting should be done only by those whom God has especially gifted for this purpose.

In the last chapter we discussed the life cycle of churches. While we looked at nuances to the various stages, there basically are just four stages in the life cycle of all organizations. The first phase is "startup." During this period, beginnings are occurring. The church is being birthed, the initial people are being gathered, the "DNA" of the future church is being incubated. The second phase, "expansion," builds on the groundwork created by the first phase. As a result, the church grows both numerically and spiritually. Buildings are constructed and organizational structure is developed in response to the ministry objectives of the new group. In the third phase, the church enters a plateau. Ministry is maintained, but the church ceases to grow. It is now a mature church. Finally, phase four occurs and the church enters the period of decline. Momentum can no longer be maintained, losses start occurring, and the church ceases to be effective in its ministry.

While this is true for churches, it is also the design of all organizations. Even businesses, towns, cities, etc., will go through this life cycle. However, business has recognized that a different kind of leader is needed for each stage of the life cycle. The gifts and talents of the person chosen to start the business are different from the qualities needed for the declining phase of the business. In fact, business will change the leaders as the organization enters a new phase, because the old leader will no longer be as effective in the new environment. So the energetic leader who starts the business is replaced by a leader who has the ability to expand it as far as possible. Once that is accomplished, a third leader is chosen to maintain the business at its maximum potential. Finally, when profit can no longer be sustained at optimal levels, a fourth leader arrives who has the ability to eke out all the profit possible from the business during the declining phase. And when profit is no longer possible, the business is closed.

Perhaps the church can learn from business. Instead of assuming that all leaders are identical, it would be more profitable to attempt to match a leader with the period of the life cycle the church is currently experiencing. Thus, pastors who have been gifted by God for maintaining an existing church should not be placed in a church planting situation. Likewise, pastors whom God has gifted for church planting will be miserable attempting to maintain an existing organization.

Church planting literature has identified four kinds of church leaders. Each kind corresponds with one of the phases of the life cycle. The first kind of church leader is identified as a "catalyzer." This gifted leader is able to take the church from nothing and come up with its most basic ingredient: people. In fact, such leaders are usually able to get the church up to around one hundred members, and then if they continue leading the church, it usually faces a quick decline. A catalytic leader has a lot of ups and downs and can easily be discouraged.

Catalytic leaders should probably be moved when they reach a high, before the church begins to go down. These leaders can continue raising up more new churches. The catalytic leader is good for the short term but not for the long haul. In fact, this kind of leader is very difficult for most conference presidents to manage. They don't know what to do with them, because they keep moving to new locations, rarely staying over two years in one place in the existing pastoral system. Most full-time evangelists are catalyzers. That's why they are so effective as evangelists, and many times so ineffective as localized pastors.Their gifts tend to make them entrepreneurial.

The catalytic leader makes an excellent church planter. In fact, evangelists who get tired of moving every six weeks for a new campaign and would like to settle down could be placed in church planting. Instead, most of them, while raising their children, settle down in a pastorate. This experience is often frustrating not only to them but to the congregation. How much better to place them in church planting, where they could spend one or two years raising up a church and then move on to a new plant. It would provide the evangelist with stability and also greatly enhance the witness of the church.

The second kind of church leader is the organizer. This person is able to pick up where the catalyzer leaves off. The leader helps people find their niche in the church so that everything can run smoothly. While the catalyzer is short on organizational skills, the organizer experiences a "heyday." People are being organized, spiritual gifts are discovered, and people are being placed into ministry. Things really start to happen, and the church enters an excellent growth phase under this person's leadership. This type of leader may not be able to get a church started from nothing, but he or she has the ability to organize that initial group so that growth really occurs. When everything is finally organized and running smoothly, the organizer gets bored and is ready to move on for a deeper challenge. The skills of both the catalyzer and the organizer are needed for successful church plants. If the church planter is a catalyzer but does not have organizational skills, a replacement will need to be made within the first two years of the birth of the church. However, some individuals have been highly gifted by God to be both a catalyzer and an organizer. These individuals make good "founding pastors" of new churches because they can get the church up and going and also help it expand. Such giftedness is somewhat rare today. Perhaps as the church continues to move in the direction of being a church planting movement, God will give the church more people gifted to be catalytic-organizers.

Another possibility in church planting is to create a team. (Remember, Jesus said they should be sent out two by two.) In such a church planting team, one person would be a catalyzer and the other an organizer. This would enable them to support each other in their giftedness and both could stay by the new church much longer. Paul was probably a catalytic organizer, and God greatly used him to plant many successful churches.

The third kind of leader is the "operator." This is the leader who is gifted to maintain the status quo (when it is good). The person tries not to mess up what has been created and keeps the church running smoothly. These are multi-planning people, who know how to operate what is already going well. The majority of pastors have been trained to be operators—replacement pastors of existing churches. These are not bad leaders—the church needs a host of them to keep the existing churches alive—but these leaders would rarely make good church planters.

The fourth kind of leader has been dubbed the "developer." These persons specialize in attempting to turn a declining church around. In a sense, they are similar to the catalyzers, and their characteristics are somewhat similar, but their main focus is on existing churches rather than starting new ones. Developers come in two categories. First are the restorers who are able to pick up a church when it is heading downhill and recreate a church that is alive, healthy, and reproducing. The second are the terminators whom God has gifted to bring closure to an existing congregation. Some churches have finished their life cycle and need to be buried with dignity. They can celebrate what God has done through them, but realize that time has come to pass the "torch" to a new generation of churches. Many churches continue, knowing that death is inevitable. Some are sustained on life support systems that prevent them from dying gracefully. They are "vegetables" but continue to maintain the form. Perhaps God has gifted some leaders to bring successful termination to the life of what has been a great church, but whose life cycle has now ended.

Those who are selecting people for church planting need to make careful assessments of a person's leadership skills to ensure that the right kind of a leader is selected. Catalyzers and organizers make the best church planters. Before selecting a person as a church planter or before one feels that God has called them to church plant, an assessment of their leadership qualities ought to be done. Most church planting failures occur because of the wrong choice of a leader. Nothing is more important than choosing the right person for the church plant.

Characteristics of Church Planters

A few years ago a small group of Adventists interested in church planting met with a consultant. This professional began by leading us through a process of deciding what a well-planted Seventh-day Adventist church would look like. We ultimately came up with this definition:

A Well-Planted Seventh-day Adventist Church Manifests:

• A strong, passionate vision for reaching the lost, as well as

- Unconditional love and acceptance of people everywhere

Organizes So That

- Every believer is cared for and grows
- Every member is released for ministry, and
- Its resources are focused on winning the lost

Creates Public Services

- Where seekers are attracted to Christ
- Where believers are renewed by vibrant worship of Christ
- Where believers are encouraged as they grow in Christ while valuing our Adventist heritage and theology.

Having arrived at this definition, the consultant next led our group to decide what kind of characteristics would be needed in the ideal church planter in order to plant this kind of church. The group settled on five professional skills and five personal skills that would absolutely be needed in a church planter.

The first of the five professional skills is to be a *visionary*. A church planter must be able to possess a vision of what God has called the new church to accomplish and be able to articulate it to a significant number of people. The second professional skill is *leadership*. Having been granted a vision of God's leading, the church planter must also be a leader of people. A leader is defined as "one who has followers." Leaders can be good or bad, but one cannot be a leader without followers.

The third skill needed is *evangelism*. It is not sufficient to be able to galvanize a group of people and get them excited about starting a church. The church planter must also be an evangelizer. If our desire was to simply plant churches by redistributing the saints, then this characteristic would be unnecessary, but since the focus of our church planting is to be harvest-centered, the church planter must be a winner of souls. If the church planter does not win souls, then neither will the flock. No one who is not a soul winner should ever be invited to plant a church. A desire to win souls should never be confused with the ability to do so. Evidence of that ability should be demanded before anyone is granted the support of the church for church planting. Non-soul-winning church planters will produce after their kind.

The fourth skill is *communication*. Since so much of ministry depends on the ability to communicate accurately, it is of vital necessity that the church planter be a good communicator. This is a skill that can be easily researched, so that those evaluating will know that the person being considered for church planting has demonstrated the ability to communicate well, both through preaching and teaching, and in internal communication with other members and staff.

The fifth skill is *a knowledge of church planting*. There is certain basic information that should be known before one begins the church planting process. This knowledge can be gained through extensive reading, taking an academic course in church planting, or attending some of the Seeds Conferences. Familiarity with modern research on church planting will enable the individual to avoid many of the pitfalls that the planter would otherwise have to learn through trial and error.

In addition to these professional skills, the group also identified five personal skills that should be present in the ideal Adventist church planter. The first is *relational*. While relational skills are important for any type of ministry, they are of particular importance for church planting. In an existing church, the pastor has a ready-made family, waiting for the pastor's arrival. However, in a church plant, there is no one waiting. If people don't like the planter, they won't stay around. Relational skills are needed to gather the initial group of Adventists who will form the nucleus and are also needed in order to begin reaching out and becoming friends with people in the community.

The second personal skill, *character,* is absolutely foundational. A church planter need not be a saint, but must not have glaring character flaws. If there are flaws of a moral or financial nature in the character, they will be exposed very quickly under the stress of church planting. Investigation into the character reputation of the proposed church planter is essential before an investment is made.

The third personal skill needed is *family solidarity.* The pressures of church planting can easily fracture any marital relationship that does not have a strong foundation. Many church planters have shipwrecked their families because this problem was not noted before they began the church plant. Church planting is a lonely profession, especially for the spouse. That is why a support system for church planters is so essential. None should enter church planting whose marriage is not rock solid.

The fourth personal skill needed is *emotional stability.* Since church planters experience many lonely times, those whose emotions are unstable could easily become discouraged. There are many "highs" in church planting, but between those "highs" are a lot of "lows." If one cannot endure the "lows," he or she will never experience the "highs." Church planters should not depend too much on others or manipulate others to accomplish their goals.

The final personal skill is *prayer and spirituality.* This has not been left to last because it is the least important, but because it is the most important. Surveys of church planters have continually revealed that prayer is the most essential ingredient in the life of the church planter. In the next chapter we will discuss the importance of prayer, but here our emphasis is not the corporate prayer of the church, but the personal prayer life of the planter. Spiritual, praying planters will produce spiritual, praying churches.

In addition to these very basic characteristics, there are several other competencies that need to be exhibited in the life of the church planter. The planter needs to be a self-starter. No one is going to be checking on the planter every day to see that the job is being accomplished. People who need someone to hold them accountable on a regular basis should not become church planters.

Furthermore, the church planter needs to be adaptable and flexible. One may approach church planting with a well-thought-out plan, but one which in reality does not work well. Good church planters will quickly recognize that and will constantly switch plans and ways of working as they interact with the people they are trying to reach. For this reason, younger people usually make better planters than older people, since they are more flexible by nature. The older a person becomes, the more inflexible they tend to become. Of course, there is always the exception.

A church planter must have good self-esteem. A person who does not have a sense of self-worth is not likely to become a good church planter. When low-self-esteem people attempt a church plant that fails, the result will be to lower their self-esteem even more. A church planter needs to convey faith that God can do something magnificent and great through the people that are coming together to raise up the new church. The church planter is the key to creating faith in the group that is planting the new church.

A final characteristic is church loyalty. If the church to be planted is Seventh-day Adventist, then the planter must be fiercely loyal to the supporting church. That loyalty must be seen in the desire to plant a church which is true to Seventh-day Adventist beliefs and doctrines. Adventists believe that God brought them into existence and entrusted them with a special message of truth for earth's last hour. The multitudes must be reached with the real thing, not a compromised version of the message.

Within Adventism there have always been wide differences on the nonessentials, but there has always been, at the same time, unswerving loyalty to the pillars of the church. Planters may differ in methodology, but they must have no questions about the pillars of the Adventist faith. In assessing church planters, this is one area that must never be overlooked or disaster is already on the horizon for the new church. The history of the church has been littered by the "great" preachers who thought they could plant great churches by leaving the Adventist fold.

Coupled with loyalty to the teachings of the church must be real cooperation between the church planter and the local conference in whose territory the church is being planted. In Adventism we do not plant independent churches—all churches are part of the sisterhood of churches in a given conference.Therefore, one does not simply plant a church without consultation with the local conference. Individuals who are known for working independently of the conference should be carefully screened before being supported in their church planting efforts.

Assessment

Everything in this chapter thus far has been written to make one very important statement: Every person who is to be supported as a church planter must first of all be assessed. The assessment must be thorough, especially evaluating the characteristics needed in a church planter as have been outlined in this chapter. The Adventist church already has in place a church planting assessment process. Conferences can send individuals to the assessment center for evaluation. The four-day assessment process is perhaps the strongest determiner of whether a person should enter church planting.

The assessment center serves two purposes. First, it is for those individuals who are wondering if God has gifted them for church planting .They desire to be assessed for that calling. They go through the assessment process in order to discover for themselves if they are called to plant churches. Secondly, the assessment process enables conferences to discover if an individual should church plant before the conference invests thousands of dollars in the church planting project for this person.

Sending individuals, both lay people and pastors, to assessment is probably the best indicator of success in the future church plant. Utilizing people who are recommended through the assessment center will result in more successful church plants. The assessment process is not 100 percent guaranteed, but successful church plants occur in higher percentages when the recommendations of the assessment center are followed.

What happens in the assessment process? First, an individual applies for admittance to assessment. A telephone interview follows. If the initial interview is favorable, the individual is sent several forms and personality tests to complete, and recommendations are sought and evaluated. Then the person is invited to come to assessment. If problems are discovered during the initial investigation, the person would not be invited to the assessment.

The actual assessment process requires four days of intensive activity. A group of assessors is present, usually one for each couple being assessed. The assessors observe the candidates in actual ministry functions among themselves, such as preaching, conducting groups tasks, participation in groups, as well as evangelism. Personal interviews are conducted with each couple. Each evening the assessors spend additional hours together sharing what they observed and seeking consensus with regard to each candidate. Finally, on the last day, the assessors will reach a final consensus on the evaluation of each candidate's potential for church planting and will share the recommendation with the candidate and the sponsoring conference.

The assessment process is not an easy task, either for the assessed or the assessors, but it is the best indicator of the person's future performance in the ministry of church planting. It will reveal whether or not the person has the necessary professional and personal skills needed to be successful in church planting.

Church planting assessments are held several times throughout the year. Application to attend must be made several months prior to the assessment because of all the prework which needs to be done. Information on the next assessment and how one can apply can be found on the NADEI web site: *www.nadei.org.* Just look in the church planting section under assessment. If web site availability is not possible, call NADEI at (616) 471-9220 to receive information.

Where Do We Find Church Planters?

When one examines the qualities needed in a church planter, the immediate concern is, Where is the church going to find these people? These are not the qualities found in the majority of clergy being hired today. However, people enter the ministry based on what they envision ministry to be. Since our current demand is for maintenance-oriented pastors, those who are gifted in that area tend to be the ones who decide to enter the clergy ranks. If, on the other hand, the church starts utilizing entrepreneurial types, these more aggressive people will be attracted into clergy ranks. These high-energy people, gifted with the skills needed for church planting, do not currently have a challenging place in traditional clergy role. Hence many of them opt for some other calling.

If Adventism is to be a church planting movement, then the church must begin to attract significant numbers of qualified church planters. There is a temptation to search for these planters among the current members of clergy. They will not be found there in sufficient numbers to create the huge number of new churches needed. Where then does the church find these church planters?

Jesus told us what to do when we once realized the hugeness of the harvest. Matthew 9:38 declares that we should pray to the Lord of the harvest to send forth these workers. It sounds so simple that few take it seriously, yet this is the command of Jesus in view of the harvest. Please note, however, that such prayers rarely go up to God until the church really begins to see the vast harvest that God has prepared.[2] If God has commanded us to go forth and plant churches, He will provide the needed workers for the accomplishment of His commands. Remember that such churches are established for the sake of reaching the harvest and not for the redistribution of the saints. The kind of leaders we are to pray for are those who will plant churches in view of the vast harvest that God has prepared.

Ellen White has also pointed out a source for church planters: "As churches are established, it should be set before them that it is even from among them that men must be taken to carry the truth to others, and raise up new churches."[3] The vast majority of those who will plant hundreds of new Adventist churches are not even Seventh-day Adventists today. They are out in the harvest fields, waiting to be gathered in. Interestingly, Ellen White indicates that new converts will make good church planters. That is probably because their evangelistic zeal is much higher. They will need training, and they may need to be placed in a team with someone experienced in Adventism, but God's counsel is to use them. The harvest will produce more harvesters.

A church planting movement demands that the Adventist church be continually investing in training new leaders. Wise pastors and evangelists will immediately spot potential leaders from their harvest-gathering. Leadership training should begin immediately, not as formal academic training in leadership, but "on the job" training. People ought already to demonstrate leadership ability before they are sent to the seminary. The seminary should train only those who have already demonstrated that they are reproductive leaders.

The apostle Paul made this clear: "And the things which you have heard from me in the presence of many witnesses, these entrust to faithful men, who will be able to teach others also."[4] The apostle Paul enunciates that it is more important to win a *soul winner* than a *soul*. If the church is to become a reproduction system, it must develop leaders who will raise up new leaders. Thus, every person won to Christ must in turn reach someone else, who will reach another, etc. Likewise, the characteristic of true biblical leadership is that a leader will train a leader, who will train a leader, etc.

Only then can the North American church plant significant numbers of new churches and have adequate leadership for the accomplishment of that task.

Ideally, people who are not reproductive leaders should never be called into the clergy ranks. This means that calls are not extended to people who have not already produced another leader or won another soul to Christ. It is sometimes difficult to accomplish this while at seminary; therefore, individuals should demonstrate reproduction before attending seminary. Following this pattern will attract a new breed of clergy and is a first step in creating the leadership necessary for a reproductive system.

Bob Logan, noted church planting authority, suggests several places to look for candidates for church planting.[5] First, he suggests looking at pastors who bombed out in their first pastorates. Obviously, not all who bomb out will become good church planters, but if they failed because they were catalytic leaders and were frustrated by the slow pace of the maintenance-oriented church, they may be good candidates for church planting. The catalytic leader is extremely frustrated in the typical first district. Usually administration tries to settle these people down and transform them into leaders who can be satisfied with the status quo. It would be more fruitful to place such pastors into church planting, where their catalytic skills and gifts would enable them to function at peak performance. Instead, administrators and catalytic pastors both generally burn out, and with mutual agreement these individuals drop out of the ministry.

Logan suggested, as another source for church planters, seminary students with poor attendance records. This needs a little explanation. What Logan had in mind was students who missed classes because they were too busy doing ministry. Involvement in ministry was a greater priority to them than academic achievement. Such students are a frustration to the seminary, and they need the discipline the seminary offers, but hiring conferences would be well pleased to place such students into church planting situations.

Logan further suggested as a source for church planters, people who are members in large churches who create trouble and ask a lot of questions. These people are also a great frustration to the current leadership of the church. Now, some people are really trouble-makers, and these definitely should not be church planters. However, there are people with great leadership ability who are not being challenged in the presence of many other great leaders in the large church. They may even turn down leadership positions offered because they feel they are wasting time in the current situation. They are probably entrepreneurial and need to be working in something new. Many times the church loses such people because their gifts for starting something new go unrecognized and they are not trained for that ministry. Instead, they are viewed as troublemakers, and everyone breathes a sigh of relief when they finally leave.

Training for Church Planting

We have looked at sources for potential church planters. In this final section of the chapter we will quickly examine a training program for church planters, once they are selected. What is offered here is suggestive and not exhaustive. In fact, one cannot use the same training process for all potential church planters. The point we raise here is simply that they must receive some kind of preparation for their work as church planters.

The first step, obviously, in providing training for a potential church planter, would be to send the candidate to the assessment center to be evaluated by independent observers. They will recommend the person for church planting, or will recommend with qualifications. Many of those qualifications will have to do with training yet needed.

If the person has a college degree, he or she could then be sent to seminary. Currently, the Adventist seminary is mission-minded and is producing church leaders who are interested in the harvest. Sometimes this new kind of leader gets frustrated in current ministry contexts, and would function best in a church planting situation. In the past, many administrators viewed the seminary as a place where candidates for ministry lost their evangelistic zeal. That is no longer the case. Today the seminary is implanting mission and evangelism into the very psyche of the student. It may be that the seminary will need to further its enhancement of church planting by creating a church planting track. The seminary will respond to the needs of the field if the field makes it clear that it will hire people as church planters. Currently, every Master of Divinity student is required to take course work in church planting, and many seminarians attend the annual Seeds Conferences.

However, more than academic training is needed for church planters. Having graduated from seminary, the students must be placed under supervising pastors who will further enhance the seminarians' church planting skills. Much evangelistic zeal is lost when the young neophytes leave seminary and enter the internship under pastors who fail to adequately develop their skills. This evangelistic fervor is further dampened when young pastors are placed in a district where nothing is happening or has happened, and where no one expects anything to happen.The ultimate result is that whatever the new pastors try doesn't work, and they decide that all they learned in seminary doesn't work in the real world. Such experiences color the professional life of many pastors, so that even when they arrive in a district where something should happen, it doesn't, because in their mindset, "nothing works."

Instead, place the new pastors in church planting situations, where help is provided through regular coaching from experienced church planters. Let these new pastors learn while doing, not on their own, but under the tutelage of experienced planters. In fact, such a model also would be enhanced if some of the young pastors' seminary training were done while in the actual ministry context. Currently, the seminary is studying ways to bring the M.Div. curriculum out to the field.

The training spoken of here has primarily referred to clergy who will plant churches, but what about the training of lay church planters? If the Adventist Church is to be a lay movement, it must also successfully train and mobilize a vast army of lay church planters. They, too, must be assessed. However, they will not be able to receive the same extensive training that is given to the clergy person.

What can be done? Once the lay church planters have been identified and assessed, they should be assigned reading on the subject of church planting. They should be enrolled in a training program for church planting, offered in each conference or union. This training program should include brief courses in Adventist beliefs, polity, history, evangelistic methodology, and church planting. These courses could be taught by mission-driven pastors and administrators, or perhaps the seminary could develop a certification program offered in different parts of the field that would bring some of the seminary education to these potential lay pastors. A seminary course in church planting is currently available through distance education.

Lay pastors will need both training and consistent monitoring and coaching as they get involved in the church planting process. It is not a matter of trusting them or not trusting them; rather, it is a matter of supplying them with the needed support to make certain that these lay planters are successful and plant truly great Adventist churches.

Since this is an area not yet developed in Adventism, continual study will need to be given to ascertain how best to proceed. What is offered here is only suggestive of a place to begin talking and developing the needed training. If the Adventist church is serious about becoming a reproductive movement, it must give earnest attention to this training process. The important thing is not what is done in training, but that *something* is done to adequately train a whole new generation of potential church planters.

Notes:

1. Ellen G. White, *Medical Ministry*, 315.

2. See chapter one.

3. Ellen G. White, *Christian Service*, 61.

4. 2 Timothy 2:2 (NASB).

5. The author heard these remarks in a class with Dr. Robert Logan at Fuller Theological Seminary.

7

Ways to Start New Churches

In this chapter we wish to explore the different avenues through which new churches can form, as well as some of the various models being developed today. Before planting begins, it must be determined how to start the church, as well as the kind of church that will be established.

Hiving Off

Most Adventist churches are conceived by "hiving off." In this model a nucleus is formed in the mother church before moving out and becoming a new church. This model works well for redistributing the saints, but it may not be the most effective model for planting a church out of the harvest. In this model nearly 100 percent of the new church is composed of the existing church.

The problems with this model are threefold. First, the new church is usually a clone of the existing church and does not increase the variety of churches needed to reach the multifaceted harvest. Second, this model frightens the existing church because it takes away so many members. Third, many times this model fails to impact its community significantly because it is mainly composed of members from the mother church.

Yet, this model is not all bad. A new church *is* established, and while it may not reach significant numbers in the harvest, the new church will probably reach more people than the older church would have all by itself. Since this model is perceived as the only model for most Adventist churches, it is imperative that we discover other venues that can be effective for planting harvest-centered churches.

Colonization

The second suggestion for starting new churches has been called "colonization." In this model, several families move into an unentered area for the purpose of raising up a new church. This model was used extensively in early Adventism and is one that Ellen White consistently advocated. She counseled many early Adventists not to colonize in Battle Creek but to move to an area where there were no Adventists and raise up a church. This model requires sacrifice on the part of the families that move to the new location and have to find new jobs and homes. Yet the priority of the advancement of the kingdom motivates these individuals to make the needed sacrifice in order that a new church might be established.

For many people, this model conjures up the idea of people moving to some small town where there is no Adventist presence, since most large cities have an Adventist church. This model does not necessarily imply such movement. Far more important than the placement of Adventist churches in small unentered towns is the evangelization of the large cities of North America. While not neglecting the evangelization of rural America, Adventism must recapture the cities for Christ. This model does envision people moving to a large city where a new church needs to be established. In some cases there may be Adventist churches in the vicinity already, but the newly planted church will focus on reaching people who are untouched by the existing churches.

To avoid loneliness, ideally several families should enter the colonization project together. These families would provide a good nucleus to begin the new church. However, this new church is not to be composed simply of the nucleus who have moved to the new area; they must reach out and establish the new church out of the harvest.

Accidental Parenthood

The third model for starting a new church has been called "accidental parenthood." A new church was not planned, but it happened. Perhaps there was a church split or other crisis that caused the formation of a new church. Obviously, this is not the best way to start a new church. Yet God has been able to use even a church split to His glory by bringing a new church into existence out of a potentially bad situation. In fact, many church splits occur simply because the mother church is "overly pregnant" and refuses to give birth.

This way of starting a church is very challenging. Because it was not formed to reach the harvest, it is easy for this new church to focus inward. The uniting force has been the common enemy, the mother church. Once that problem has dissipated, the members may begin to fight among themselves. That's why it is imperative for this new church to begin immediately to focus on the harvest. This may be difficult, but it is the only avenue for this church to become healthy.

Many Adventist churches have been formed through the Accidental Parenthood method. How much better, however, to plant a church before the new baby splits open the womb. Newly planted churches in other models will produce less trauma, both to the mother church and to the new baby. Don't be afraid to let the baby out of the womb.

Partnership

Another model that fits well with Adventism is the partnership model. In this situation, two or three churches join together to plant one new church. Rather than "hiving off" from one existing church, this model envisions people from several churches joining together to form the nucleus of a new church. This allows small churches to plant a church without decimating their ranks. Another advantage is that the new church is less likely to be a carbon copy of the mother church, since more than one mother church is supplying the "DNA." Church planting does not attempt to clone an existing church but to plant something entirely new. This model has potential for allowing that to happen.

The above models are the primary ones whereby a mother church plants totally autonomous churches. There are ways in which a mother church can plant a new church without necessarily cutting the "apron strings." These models envision planting churches that are semi-autonomous.

Scattered Satellites

The first semi-autonomous model is called "scattered satellites." This is a model that Adventists have rarely used, yet it has tremendous potential. It is especially helpful for churches who are afraid to plant for fear of losing too many members. In this version the mother church plants several branches in various parts of a town. These branches are still part of the mother church—they just meet in different locations. For example, Metropolitan Seventh-day Adventist Church was initially planted back in the 1950s. It has been very successful, with a large membership throughout the years. As people moved out to the suburbs, the church toyed with the idea of moving to the suburbs, but that would have alienated much of its current membership. Instead, the church decided to plant a branch in the north suburbs. The members of the branch would still be members of Metropolitan but would meet in the north campus. Eventually, the Metropolitan Seventh-day Adventist Church placed four of these satellite churches around the city. The result was that the Metropolitan Church continued to grow at an accelerated rate.

This model is similar to a university with several campuses. It is one church with one pastoral staff; it just meets in different locations. It has several advantages for Adventists. It is similar to our district alignment, except that in the district there are separate, independent churches served by the same pastoral staff. The scattered satellite model has the advantage of being a very large church offering multiple options for people, yet still maintaining the closeness of a small church. It literally has the advantage of being a large and small church at the same time.

Churches that are afraid of planting should consider this model seriously. In this way they will not lose any members, but will be able to extend the kingdom of God. The church operates out of one budget but has special allocations for the satellites. The pastoral staff may serve the whole church, but it is best if someone is assigned to the satellite. In this model, the building would cease to be a barrier to the growth of the church, since the church could plant new satellites when it ran out of space.

While it was intended under this model that the new plant would remain a part of the mother church, it should be recognized that as time goes on, the satellite might desire to become autonomous. A healthy mother church will graciously accept the independent status of the new congregation. This method is less traumatic for the mother church than the loss of people to a new, independent congregation. It allows for a slower transition process if the new congregation eventually does become autonomous.

Gathered Satellites

A variation of the "scattered satellite" model is the "gathered satellite." Rather than plant new congregations in different locations, this model sees new congregations being planted within the existing building. There may be two or three different groups meeting in one church building at the same time. This model has been used fairly well within Adventism, especially for starting work with a new ethnic group.

An example of this is the church where I recently conducted an evangelistic meeting, during which we baptized a couple of Spanish people into a small English-speaking church. This forward-thinking congregation decided to conduct separate services each week for the new Spanish group. Within a few weeks, attendance of the Spanish group had grown to more than thirty. Now two congregations are meeting in the same building every Sabbath, and they are all part of one church. This model has tremendous potential for planting ethnic congregations within existing churches.

In time the ethnic church may outgrow the present facility and desire to separate to a new location, but this model has provided a nice place to incubate the new church without a lot of expense. A variation of this model would be for the two congregations to become independent but continue to share the building. A good financial contract would need to be drawn up between the two groups to avoid misunderstandings, but becoming independent might be a first step toward moving out on their own.

Multiple Services

One additional model for a mother church to use in planting a new congregation is for the mother church to add a service on Sabbath morning. This is a variation of the above model, and one with great potential in Adventism. Some may feel that starting a new service is not church planting, but churches that conduct multiple services will testify that each service attracts a different group of people, and individuals are usually faithful in attending the same service and rarely move from one to the other. Thus, in all reality, having two or three services is the same as having two or three different churches. Financially it makes a lot more sense, especially with the high cost of property and building costs today. Multiple uses of expensive property makes good stewardship sense.

Adventist churches that are successfully holding two services today usually tailor each service to a different crowd. Providing multiple options attracts more people than the church would attract with one large service. Most churches only consider going to two services because of crowded conditions. That may have been true in generations past, but today a second service is offered not because of overcrowding, but to attract different kinds of people to the church.

One Sabbath I visited a church that held three services. This church has a membership of around 700 and an attendance of 500, and operates out of a building which seats only 200. The early service was very traditional. The second service was called a "family service" and was a mild mix of the contemporary and the traditional. At the same time that the second service was being held in the sanctuary, another service, totally contemporary, was occurring in the fellowship hall. This church was attempting to meet the needs of many different kinds of people in worship style. All services were true to Adventist principles but offered different approaches to worship.

Interestingly, attendance at the contemporary service was not all youth or young adults. Many "gray heads" were present, enjoying the contemporary form of worship. In fact, there was a good mix of ages in all three services, although the contemporary service had the greatest concentration of younger people.

While it may be true in a general sense that younger people prefer the more contemporary approach to worship, it would be a mistake to assume that all young people prefer the contemporary style. Many of them actually prefer the traditional, and many older folk prefer the contemporary. In planning various kinds of services, realize that each service will be attended by a mix of ages but will also attract a specific generation in greater concentration. In the above church, the early service attracted primarily Builders or Seniors; the family service, Boomers; and the contemporary service, Gen Xers.

What time should the second service begin? That varies with the congregation, but most who conduct multiple services successfully do not start the early service too early. The preferred starting time for the early service seems to be some-

where around 8:45 a.m. to 9:00 a.m., with the second service commencing around 11:15 a.m. to 11:30 a.m. Sabbath
School usually occurs between the two services. Years ago
most churches felt that they could not hold a service over
the noon hour. That taboo has now been broken because of
churches that have gone to a second service and spilled over
the noon hour, some going as late as 1:00 p.m. This has
appealed to younger people who like to sleep in on Sabbath
morning or who have small children who are difficult to get
ready in time for a 9:30 Sabbath School.

Few Adventist churches have tried a third service. Those
who do usually hold it in another location as did the church
mentioned above. However, if adequate Sabbath School
space is available, the church could actually operate two Sabbath Schools and three worship services, provided the sanctuary is not needed for Sabbath School. The concern here is
adequate staffing for three services and two Sabbath Schools.
However, involving more people would improve the health
of the church. One of the problems with large churches is
that they do not provide enough places for people to get
involved. Operating multiple services would increase the
opportunity for involvement.

Another possibility with a third service is to conduct a Fri-
day night or early Saturday evening service. Several Adventist
churches have been successful with the early Saturday night
service, especially gearing it to seekers or new people. There
is nothing extra sacred about the hours of 11:00 and 12:00
on Sabbath morning. Other parts of the Sabbath can be used
equally well to conduct services, and each service will reach
a different group of people.

There are multiple options available for churches desir-
ing to extend the kingdom by planting a new church. As
your church prays about starting a new church, consider one
of these options and attempt a church plant. Additional services may not show up in statistical reports as new churches
planted , but nevertheless they *are* new churches that will
reach a greater harvest for Christ.

Models of Church Planting Not Involving a Mother Church

While the above models have all included a mother church in the planting process, the following models envision churches being planted without the involvement of a mother church. This is not to say that motherless models are preferable—they simply provide additional options for starting churches.

Catalytic Church Planter

This kind of church planter was referred to in the previous chapter. It is an individual who specializes in church planting. This person has all the characteristics of the catalyst, but specializes in church planting rather than full-time public evangelism. Such a person could prove helpful to many conferences who desire to see multiple churches planted. This person could be hired to move to an area for just one or two years, raise up a church, turn it over to someone else, and then go elsewhere to start another new church. Successful people here could become very adept at church planting. They would virtually devote most of their professional life to church planting. They would also have stability because they would spend at least one year in each location. In large metropolitan areas, they could conceivably spend a professional lifetime just starting churches in one metropolitan area and never need to move. There is that kind of need in most of the major megaplexes of North America.

Founding Pastor

The founding pastor is an individual hired by the conference to raise up a church and then continue as the pastor of the new church. Individuals for whom this is to be the assignment need to have the characteristics of both the catalyst and the organizer if they are going to be successful in raising up the new church and staying by to pastor it. These individuals may work with existing churches but are not dependent on them. They are hired for the specific purpose of raising up the new church. In fact, the existing churches may be oblivious to the need of a new church to reach the harvest, but the conference, sensing the great need, moves in to establish a church even when the existing churches are not excited about the adventure.

A recent seminary graduate was asked to serve as the founding pastor of a new church in a major metropolitan area. The existing churches saw no need for the new church and offered little support to the new group. Since the conference had sent the new pastor there, he began his work with just his own family. Slowly, by visiting the existing churches, he won tolerance and a handful of people to help. In less than a year he had as many as sixty people attending church each week, most of them coming from the harvest.

Church Planting Teams

This model of church planting is a variation of the previous two models. The main difference is that instead of an individual church planter or a founding pastor, the conference hires a team of two or three people to begin the new church. This is a highly preferable way to start churches, but is used very little among Adventists because of the high cost of multiple salaries with no tithe base at startup. This is purely an adventure in faith.

The advantages of this model are obvious. The team members can support each other, which will solve the problem of isolation that most church planters feel. Multiple leaders provide diverse qualities. The team therefore should be made up of individuals who enhance one another with their strengths. Ideally, one should be a catalyst and the other an organizer, and if there is a third, that person could be an operator.

The team approach is expensive, but it is one that Jesus advocated and the early church practiced. If conferences could do some realignment along the lines suggested in chapter three of this work, enough money would be saved to follow the counsel of Jesus and allow teams to work together to start new churches. This method of church plant-ing should primarily be used where a conference desires to plant a major new church. It would not be financially fea-sible for small church plants.

Independent Church Planter

This model differs from the others primarily in the fact that the planter is not hired by the conference but works in close consultation with them. The planter probably is a lay-person. It is not expected that this person will ever be hired by the conference.

This model is used primarily by those who wish to estab-lish lay churches without paid pastors. These churches will send their tithes to the local conference but do not expect the conference to supply a pastor, since they are able to care for themselves. This model would resemble early Adventism and would primarily be used in the planting of small churches, although some larger churches may use this model. Also, at some future time the church started by an indepen-dent church planter may eventually be placed in the hands of a pastor who is hired by the conference.

This is another model with tremendous potential for Adventists. The biggest negative for the conference would be the lack of control of the church planter, since no salary is paid. However, the conference could appoint the leader who would be held accountable through regular interaction with the local conference. Such individuals should go through the assessment process before a conference would give them its blessing to start a church.

Ellen White lends her support to lay people planting churches in the following statements:

> Close around us are cities and towns in which
> no efforts are made to save souls. Why should not
> families who know the present truth settle in these
> cities and villages, to set up there the standard of
> Christ, working . . . in God's way, to bring the light

before those who have no knowledge of it? . . . There will be laymen who will move into towns and cities, and into apparently out-of-the-way places, that they may let the light which God has given them shine forth to others.[1]

Brethren who wish to change their location . . . should move into towns and villages where there is little or no light and where they can be of real service and bless others with their labor and experience.[2]

Bi-Vocational Church Planter

In this model an individual is offered a small stipend to move into an area and raise up a church. The person makes the rest of his or her living by working in secular employment or by canvassing. As the church grows and the tithe base increases, the conference increases their support until the person arrives at full salary. However, some churches will never reach that point and the person will forever be a bi-vocational pastor. There is no problem with this, and the Adventist organization needs to be big enough to accommodate several part-time pastors.

There does seem to be some biblical precedent for this model. The apostle Paul seems to have operated on this model when he began most of the New Testament churches during the years of his ministry. Many churches will never get started unless this approach is tried. Smaller conferences have already attempted it with good success. They never could have afforded to hire a person full time to start a church, but the stipend approach has enabled them to successfully plant several churches without overextending their resources.

Notes:

1. Ellen G. White, *Christian Service*, 80, 81.

2. Ellen G. White, *Gospel Workers*, 52.

8

What Kind of Church Should I Plant?

When the Adventist pioneers went forth on their church planting mission, they planted churches everywhere. Little thought was given to the kind of church that they should plant. In those days there were not different kinds of churches. A church was a church. The population was fairly homogeneous, and one size basically fit all. However, the Adventist world of the twenty-first century is vastly different from the simple rural life of mid-nineteenth century America. Times have changed—and changed immensely.

When the pioneers began their massive task of carrying the three angels' messages to the world, they limped along by foot and horse. The world, however, changed in their lifetime from a simple agricultural society to a heavily industrialized society. Ellen White moved with the times and helped Adventism move from an Eastern/Midwest religion to a worldwide movement. The Adventist church moved west with the

139

development of the American west. However, by the beginning of the twentieth century, this rural migration had begun to change. Urbanization was beginning as people began moving from small rural towns to the major cities.

As Ellen White saw these phenomena, she began to urge the church to become serious about city evangelism. In fact, she spent the last fifteen years of her life attempting to get the Adventist church to change its focus and methods to reach the new America that was emerging. Adventism never succeeded in accomplishing that goal, although a start was made under the leadership of A.G. Daniells in the teen years of the twentieth century.

The industrialized age into which Ellen White attempted to move the Adventist church one hundred years ago vanished by mid-century. A new age arose. The industrialized world quickly disintegrated as America and the world moved into the computer age. In fact, the last half of the twentieth century has seen some of the most massive changes ever to occur in such a short period of time in the history of planet Earth.

Most people today work in information systems rather than industrial systems. We live not only in an information age, but also in a global society. The masses of humanity today live in dependance on each other. Stock prices falling in Asia in the late nineties impacted the entire world. This truly is a different age.

One of the most significant changes to occur in people's lives today is the vast number of choices with which they are confronted daily. Prior to the 1950s, people had a few choices, but today the options are numberless. Just look at the countless selections one faces at the supermarket in selecting cereals, sodas, toothbrushes, or deodorants, for example. Choice has become a key factor for today's society.

However, most churches today operate as if they were still living prior to 1950. They offer people only one option. That may have worked in the 1850s, but it is ineffective in the twenty-first century. How does this impact church planting? The pioneers could plant one kind of church that would satisfy everyone. But the multiplicity of choices available in today's world demands that the Adventist church offer multiple options or styles of churches. If the church wishes to be an effective agent for God in these closing days of earth's history, it must move into the twenty-first century by providing choices in church style.

As Ellen White saw the changes taking place at the beginning of the twentieth century, she urged the church to change its methodologies to reach the new populations that were emerging. If she were living today she would likewise urge the church to advance to new frontiers to reach people where they are. That was her style. That is the heritage of Adventism. To be stuck in the 1950s in methodology and church style is to be disobedient to the heritage given the Adventist church under the inspired guidance of Ellen White. We dare not be unfaithful here.

In this chapter we wish to examine the different kinds of churches that can be planted today. Yet this survey will not exhaust the possibilities. New kinds of churches will continue to be invented to reach the changing needs of the population as time tarries on planet earth. This quick survey of various church styles will help planters decide what kind of church God is calling them to plant.

The Traditional Church

Let us begin with the most familiar model. It is the one in which a pastor oversees the daily operation of the church. This church may have a pastor all to itself or it may share a pastor with several churches. (In a previous chapter we dealt with pastoral role, so in this chapter pastoral role will not be the key to understanding how church is done. The pastoral role described earlier can be used in any model of church.)

The key component in the traditional church is that it is organized around *programs*. People attend on Sabbath morning and may or may not be involved in other activities sponsored by the local church. The church usually owns or rents a building, and most activities take place there.

Some have predicted the demise of the traditional church in the new century, but it will be far from dead. However, it may be a little different, with some adjustments to make it more relevant. The need for traditional churches is sparked by a large potential harvest of people nurtured in the church, but who left the church. When they decide to come back, many of them come looking for the traditional church, because that is the church of their childhood. They can get turned off by the more contemporary services found in some of the newer churches. Thus, traditional churches will be needed to reach these returning younger generations, as well as the older generation that feels more comfortable with the traditional style.

In the traditional church the worship style is usually more formal and less participatory than in contemporary services. People sing the great hymns of the faith. Traditional, however, does not mean *boring*. To appeal to people, traditional churches must conduct their services with excellence. Traditional services can inspire those who attend and fill a real need in their lives.

The Seeker-Sensitive Church

One of the newer forms of church being developed today is the *seeker-sensitive church*. A "seeker" is defined as one who is searching out God and the church. The seeker is attempting either to come to Christ for the first time or to return to Him, having had an experience with God earlier in life. The seeker-sensitive church attempts to be sensitive to the needs of this seeker.

This kind of church encourages its members to regularly bring their friends and neighbors to church. The worship service is seen as the front door of the church, so nothing happens that will embarrass a guest. Visitors who desire to be anonymous are allowed the freedom to come and go without being hassled for name and address. The sermon has nothing in it that would be offensive to the guest. The preacher prepares the sermon with the guest in mind. Signs to restrooms and classrooms are clearly marked, and helpful greeters enable the visitors to quickly locate whatever they need.

The seeker-sensitive service is not geared to visitors, but it *is* sensitive to guests so that nothing offends people who are attending for the first time. In this church, the Sabbath School teachers are careful of their use of Spirit of Prophecy. This is not because they think less of Ellen White and her writings but because she is unknown to the visitors and they do not want her messages to be a stumbling block.

The seeker-sensitive church is a bridge between the traditional church and the seeker-driven church, which we will examine next. The seeker-sensitive church is very much like the traditional church, except that it is extremely sensitive to the needs of the seekers who happen to attend the church. The music in this style of church is apt to be a mixture of traditional hymns and contemporary music.

The Seeker-Driven Church

The third kind of church that we are examining is the *seeker-driven church*. This church is radically different from the previous two. It is totally driven by the needs of the seeker. In fact, the whole service is geared to meet the needs of the seeker. While the seeker-sensitive church attempts to meet the needs of the believer and to be sensitive to the seeker, the seeker-driven church unabashedly focuses on the needs of the seeker.

In the seeker-driven church, the entire service, from music to sermon, is geared to meet seekers where they are. The music is very contemporary, attempting to utilize a form that is familiar to unchurched people. Drama is usually a major emphasis in this kind of church. Attempting to reach people in the way that Jesus did, by telling stories about life, the seeker-driven church utilizes drama as an art form for communicating truth to the visual generation.

A worship team usually leads out in both the music and drama. There is nothing traditional about the order of service in this kind of church; in fact, the order can change week by week.

One senses, correctly, that the major difference in these first three churches centers on worship form. The seeker-driven church is contemporary in all parts of its worship service. It is designed to appeal especially to the visual generation. Thus, even the sermon is apt to be well illustrated with computer graphics. (It should be mentioned that the traditional and seeker-sensitive churches will use some of these forms once in awhile. The difference is that in the seeker-driven church, these forms define it. People come to expect these forms every week, not just on an occasional Sabbath.)

People regularly bring their friends and neighbors to seeker-driven churches. It is not surprising to see many who are not yet Adventists attending the services. Many former Adventists are also attracted to this new form of worship. Attendees in seeker-driven churches do not just sit back and enjoy the service—they actively participate. Many times they will clap their hands or even raise them before the Lord. Their worship affects their entire being, not just their cognitive nature.

The sermon in the seeker-driven church is usually Christianity 101. The preacher deliberately stays away from the deep matters of the Word of God during worship. These are usually delved into at another time. In fact, most seeker-driven churches have a "believer's service" which is more geared to fill the needs of believers. While seekers may attend, they know that this service is meant for believers, and rarely does a first-time guest attend the believer's service.

This worship concentration on seekers presents a danger that Adventists will need to avoid if they are to be successful in this model. When the seeker sermon is made the Sabbath morning service, there is a real concern that many people will never move beyond Christianity 101. It is difficult for people to attend more than one service a week on a regular basis. Since the Sabbath morning service is the first choice of most people, there is a real danger that many members of this kind of church could get stuck in Christianity 101 and never move on to maturity in the Christian life. This is a major problem that must be addressed if churches are to remain faithful to the Adventist message. While Adventism is big enough to accommodate different worship styles, we cannot tolerate a church that fails to brings its members to maturity.

One way this problem can be avoided in seeker-driven churches is to have the seeker service at some time other than Sabbath morning. Make Sabbath morning the believers' service, and perhaps conduct a Saturday evening service for seekers. Non-Adventist churches have used Sunday morning for their seeker-service. Adventist churches have had a tendency to copy the non-Adventist model and transfer their seeker service from Sunday to Sabbath morning. While the Sunday morning services work well for non-Adventist churches, since that is the time most unchurched people think of going to church, there is no such advantage for Adventists to hold a seeker service on Sabbath morning.

Saturday evening is becoming a time when people will go to church. Many Sunday-keeping churches now employ a Saturday night service. This would be easy for Adventist seeker-driven churches to do. However, some Adventist churches may wish to even consider a Sunday morning seeker service. This sounds heretical at first thought, but it was a method used by many of the early Adventists. Holding a service on Sunday morning does not deny Sabbath keeping unless one is neglecting Sabbath worship. Conducting a Sunday service to attract visitors is no different from holding an evangelistic service on Sunday night, as done by Adventists in times past. The only difference is that the service is in the morning instead of in the evening. Since Sunday evening is no longer a major church night, Saturday night or Sunday morning can work well for this seeker service.

This use of Sunday for missionary work is certainly in harmony with the counsel God has given this church. Note the evidence from both Ellen White and Adventist history. When Edson White was beginning the work among African-Americans in the southern field, he began his activity among them by conducting a Sunday school. Since Sunday schools were the primary means of entry into the church in that age, it was natural for those early Adventists to use the Sunday school in beginning new work. Ellen White commends this enterprise of Edson:

> When Edson's letters presented the work that he was doing in the Southern field by his boat, used as a meeting house, when he told of the gathering of the children for Sunday School, of the invitations he received to hold meetings, of the souls who were being interested in these meetings. . . .[1]

As Adventist work began on the great continent of Australia, Ellen White played a major role in the establishment of the work according to the divine model as she understood it. In Arthur White's biography of his grandmother, he tells how the the early Adventists in Australia first held Sunday services to reach the Sunday keepers. Later, as these people came to understand the Sabbath, they were transitioned to Sabbath worship. This is not a mandate that Sunday worship must be used as a means to attract people. However, it is clear that the early Adventists did not feel it was contrary to their strong belief in the Sabbath to hold services on Sunday.

> Many of the older students, under the direction of Brother and Sister Robinson, are working up the missionary interests in the neighborhood. Children's meetings and a Sunday school are being held at Awaba. Sabbath services and Sabbath school at Dora Creek.[2]

This practice is in harmony with all that Ellen White has counseled regarding how God's people are to use Sunday, especially at the time the Sabbath becomes a test. If it can be used for missionary work then, what is to prevent the church from using it for missionary purposes today?

> Give Sunday to the Lord as a day for doing missionary work. Take the students out to hold meetings in different places, and to do medical missionary work. They will find the people at home, and will have a splendid opportunity to present the truth. This way of spending Sunday is always acceptable to the Lord.[3]

> They [James and Ellen White] expected that their labor in Oswego would be principally for the church, but they found on arrival that handbills had been circulated through the city advertising lectures on Sabbath and Sunday.[4]

Ellen White reported fifteen hundred people attending her Sunday meetings, morning and evening:[5]

> Let the teachers in our schools devote Sunday to missionary effort. I was instructed that they would thus be able to defeat the purposes of the enemy. Let the teachers take the students with them to hold meetings for those who know not the truth. Thus they will accomplish more than they could in any other way.[6]

Using Sunday for holding evangelistic meetings, even on Sunday morning, seems to be a regular practice of both Ellen White and other early Adventists. They saw nothing that would detract from the Sabbath to use Sunday in this manner. The modern seeker service on Sunday morning would then be faithful to our Adventist heritage of using Sunday to reach people for Christ and eventually leading them into Sabbath keeping.

The Cell Church

One of the newer kinds of churches to develop in recent years has been the *cell church*. It really isn't new, for it bears close resemblance to the church of the first century. Obviously, it is organized differently from the first century church, but in principle it is very similar, having strong relational roots.

The cell church is built around relationships. While the three models previously discussed may utilize small groups, the cell church cannot exist apart from the group structure. In fact, the entire organization and operation of this kind of church is built around groups. It does not operate multiple programs as does the traditional church, or even the seeker-type churches. It does not try to attract people through its worship service, although that may happen. It focuses on reaching people through the group structure.

In the cell church, one must belong to a group in order to be a member of the church. Most new people are assimilated into a group long before they become members of the church. The groups meet weekly in the homes and offices of the community, as well as on Sabbath. The cell church does not need to own a building for worship, although it may rent a facility where all of the groups may gather for a weekly or monthly service. The facility is not important—people are. Therefore the structure of the church is based upon relationships between people.

In the cell church, if the groups don't meet together on Sabbath they will usually meet as a cell for Sabbath worship. Multiple group worship is optional. Music style is not an issue, although many cell churches will use music similar to that used in the seeker-sensitive church. However, this church is more about relationships than about musical style.

Nurture in the cell church is provided within the groups. The pastor oversees the groups but does not provide the care. Keeping the groups small (fewer than twelve people) promotes the formation of deep relational bonds within the groups. The groups are safe havens; people feel comfortable bringing their friends. Ministries also develop out of the group's placing group members in contact with the outside community.

Each cell usually sponsors a particular ministry. Cells are very mission minded—they are not closed communities. A discipleship track exists in all true cell churches. This system is designed to help a new believer come to faith in Christ, understand and accept the basic Adventist message, develop a strong prayer and Bible study life, develop the leadership potential in each individual, as well as equip the believer for ministry, including the reaching of their friends and neighbors for Christ. It is this solid plan of discipleship that is the heart and center of the cell church.

The cell church does not have regular church officers as do other churches. The structure is entirely different. In fact, the cell paradigm is so different that it is difficult for many to grasp this new way of doing church. Before embarking on a journey to begin a cell church, church planters will need considerable training into this paradigm.[7]

A few Adventist cell churches have begun to form. These experimental churches are enabling us to learn what works and what doesn't. Since the cell model is still in its embryotic stage, considerable learning must still take place. Those who are involved in cell church planting need regular communication with each other to aid in the learning process.

Since this is such an unusual kind of church, it would be most difficult to transition an existing church into this model. It is best to begin a cell church through a new church plant. The greatest danger facing cell church planters is a failure to fully understand what is involved to make this church a dynamic reality in meeting people's needs. Some have planted churches with small groups and then called them cell churches. However, simply having small groups does not make a church a cell church, especially if the discipleship track is not in place. The cell church is entirely different.

The cell church model has tremendous potential in Adventism. Since most early Adventist churches were similar to this model, our background should enable us to grasp this concept more easily than other denominations. However, we have not created this kind of church for over a hundred years, so recreating it will be slow going. Yet this is a viable alternative for church planters. Cell church is not for everyone and will not appeal to everyone. But we need these different models in order to reach the greatest number of people with the saving gospel of Jesus Christ and the three angels' messages.

Four Models

These four models of church provide at least four choices for the church planter. This does not mean that there are only four choices—other models may be developed as time goes on. In this sense, four Adventist churches planted within one mile of each other could conceivably appeal to four different kinds of people, especially if each were a different model. Remember, there are also variations within each model.

No one style of church is superior to the others. It is easy to prioritize the different kinds of churches and suggest that one is better than the others. However, the important criteria is how the model relates to the community in which it is being planted. All types can effectively reach people out of the harvest and bring them to Jesus. One of the first decisions church planters need to make is over the style of church God is calling them to plant. Once the nucleus is agreed on the type of new church to be planted, they can begin preparing for the creation of the new church.

Music

Since much of the difference between church styles, especially in the first three models, centers on music, it would be well to first examine music. Yet to do so risks alienating some on both sides of the music question. For example, there will be those who feel that I have gone too far in condoning certain musical styles in the church. On the other hand, I may alienate some who feel I have not gone far enough. The purpose of this book is to explore church planting, not musical styles. Yet one cannot ignore the variations in musical style that are available today for church planting. Nothing will divide an Adventist congregation more quickly today than a discussion of musical styles. In fact, this division is not limited to Adventist circles but is affecting most denominations today.

Because of the deep division caused by the introduction of new musical styles, it is best not to try to change the musical styles of an existing church. If one can secure agreement among the nucleus forming the new church, then it is possible to plant a new church with a different musical style.

The introduction of new musical styles and new instruments has been met by opposition in every age of the church. If only we knew the musical style of the first Christians and could copy that, we would be safe! Fortunately, we do not know what they sang or how they sang it. If we did discover and tried to copy it, it would be a great mistake. Music is an expression of culture. Various cultures display musical styles and tastes reflective of their times. To insist that only one musical style, mine, is correct is to deny the differences that exist between all groups of people.

European religious culture is indebted to the Middle Ages. There, church was a place to reverence God. A feeling of awe was created by the majesty of the divine, as displayed by the mighty cathedrals which they built. Most of the hymnody that developed during that age reflects the majesty that the age inspired. However, the majesty of God is only one aspect of God. The God of the Bible did not just sit on His ivory throne and inspire awe—He came down and lived among us. As the Reformation period began, their hymns reflected the human side of God, the Christ who lived among us and died for us. The ultimate end of this focus was the development of the gospel songs in the late nineteenth and early twentieth centuries. These songs expressed the experience of the human race in their struggle with the sin problem. Because they dealt with the experience of humanity, such gospel songs were usually written according to the secular musical style of the day. They therefore ministered to the needs of the people in the musical language that they could understand.

Contemporary music, building off the vast musical heritage of the past, has attempted to blend the two kinds of religious music. It has used the tunes and musical style of today and placed with them words that are more God-directed than were the hymns of the gospel music era. Much contemporary music, for example, uses the psalms as a basis for the song, or even uses the actual words of scripture along with a tune written in contemporary style. "Contemporary" does not mean rock music—a lot of contemporary music has been written in styles other than rock, which most churches seem to fear being brought into their midst.

Is one kind of music superior to the other? No. It all depends upon one's cultural exposure. Some are moved by classical music while others are equally moved by the more contemporary music. One is not a higher musical expression than the other. All have their appropriate use in the worship of God. Which style should you choose for your church? It all depends upon who God is calling you to reach.

I have not dealt with rock music, nor will I. I have attempted to briefly lay down some principles on musical style. Each church will have to choose the style that best fits them. At the same time, those of us who choose different styles should not condemn those who choose a style contrary to the one that we enjoy. For example, there is a real temptation for one who is using contemporary music in their worship style to chastise those using a traditional style. Such criticism of others in the Adventist family is worse than the use of any musical form they may have chosen. Musical style is not one of the twenty-seven fundamental beliefs of Seventh-day Adventists and should never be treated as such. This does not mean that all music is suitable for the church. Churches need to carefully examine the music they use and make certain that it uplifts God, but at the same time we need to guard against criticism.

What about musical instrumentation in worship? Every instrument currently used in the church, including the organ, endured severe criticism as it made its entry into the church. Our generation has accepted the organ and piano as acceptable instruments for worshiping God. In recent years we struggled with accepting the guitar in worship. Yet today that instrument is widely accepted. The current instrument of great debate is the drum. There will probably come a time when drums are so widely accepted that one would wonder how anyone could have opposed their use, but by then another instrument will be under question.

The question of instrumentation is more about the way it is played than it is about the type of instrument. For example, every academy band that plays in an Adventist church for worship brings in a drum, without any criticism, and has done so for many years. Yet bring in the drum separate from the band, and eyebrows are raised to their heights. There is nothing inherently sinful about a drum. Psalm 150 indicates clearly that all instruments can be used to praise God. No instrument is forbidden by Scripture. However, the way an instrument is played could be objectionable.

Today many churches are abandoning the organ as the instrument of choice. Fewer and fewer churches are using the organ, replacing it with the modern synthesizer. The reason is simple—the modern generation does not appreciate the organ. No matter how wonderful the organ may sound to us, the cold fact is that people today prefer other instrumentation. Back in the 1970s nearly a half million home organs were sold in the United States, but by the 1990s this figure fell to 14,000, and half of them were sold by one store in Florida. The older people are, the more likely they are to enjoy organ music. If a church is focusing on reaching the senior generation (and some churches need to), then it would be a mistake not to utilize the beautiful sounds of the organ. Yet if the focus of the church's outreach is to be younger people, then the church must choose a modern instrument which speaks in a language that the target group will understand.

Ellen White has much to say about music and instrumentation. Let's notice some of her counsel on this most difficult subject:

> Those who make singing a part of divine worship should select hymns with music appropriate to the occasion, not funeral notes, but cheerful, yet solemn, melodies.

> The hour for joyful, happy songs of praise to God and his dear Son had come.

> The singing should not be done by a few only. All present should be encouraged to join in the song service. There are times when a special message is borne by one singing alone or by several uniting in song. But the singing is seldom to be done by a few.

> Let the talent of singing be brought into the work. The use of musical instruments is not at all objectionable. They were used in religious services in ancient times. The worshipers praised God upon the harp and cymbal, and music should have its place in our services. It will add to the interest.

> I am glad to hear the musical instruments that you have here. God wants us to have them.

> Another matter which should receive attention, both at our camp meetings and elsewhere, is that of singing. . . . Organize a company of the best singers, whose voices can lead the congregation, and then let all who will, unite with them...They should devote some time to practice, that they may employ this talent to the glory of God.

> In the meetings held, let a number be chosen to take part in the song service. And let the singing be accompanied with musical instruments skillfully handled. We are not to oppose the use of instru-

ments of music in our work. This part of the service is to be carefully conducted; for it is the praise of God in song. The singing is not always to be done by a few. As often as possible, let the entire congregation join.[8]

These statements reveal that Ellen White felt strongly about music in the church. In fact, she lays down several principles in the above passages. The music used is to be joyful and happy; it is to include full participation on the part of the congregation. Musical instrumentation was to be utilized for the accompaniment of the song service. She seems to indicate that multiple instruments are to be used. Furthermore, she indicates that a song service should be conducted by not one leader but by a group of the best singers leading out with musical accompaniment.

Ellen White was against formality in worship. She was not opposed to organized worship, but to formality that was dry and lifeless. For Ellen White, worship was a vibrant experience that demonstrated clearly that Christ was a meaningful person in people's lives:

The evil of formal worship cannot be too strongly depicted, but no words can properly set forth the deep blessedness of genuine worship.[9]

God is displeased with your lifeless manner in his house, your sleepy, indifferent ways of conducting religious worship. You need to bear in mind that you attend divine service to meet with God, to be refreshed, comforted, blessed, not to do a duty imposed upon you.[10]

Adventist worship services are to be full of life and vigor. They are not to be patterned after dry formalism. Worship time ought to be a happy time. "I was glad when they said unto me, Let us go into the house of the Lord."[11] Whatever the style of worship chosen, it must have life and cause people to be happy. True believers cannot enter the presence of God and not be made infinitely happy.

Other elements being introduced into Adventist worship today, such as hand clapping and raising of hands, have also caused some concern. It is true that these elements have appeared in Pentecostal worship. However, just because Pentecostals use certain elements in worship does not necessarily make it wrong to use them. For example, Pentecostals use the Bible in worship. Should we then conclude that it is wrong to use the Bible in worship?

Some have suggested that clapping in church is directed toward the performer, but that "amen" is directed toward God. Yet one notices louder "amens" when someone performs well. Clapping or saying "amen" are cultural expressions of joy. Both have Scriptural backing. "O clap your hands, all ye people; shout unto God with the voice of triumph."[12] Scripture does not specify one kind of response only. Both are encouraged.

The problem today in most Anglo churches is that neither is done. People just sit nonresponsively. Such action must be far more repugnant to God than a response of "amen" or clapping. There are a few references to clapping in Ellen White's writings—all positive. While speaking to 15,000 people at the Groveland camp meeting, she reported the following: "I was stopped several times with clapping of hands and stomping of feet. I never had a more signal victory."[13] Evidently Ellen White enjoyed it when people clapped in response to her message and appearance. And this was at an Adventist camp meeting.

Raising of hands in worship is not a modern phenomena. It existed in Bible times as well as in early Adventism, and it is appearing once again today. There are nine biblical references to hand raising, all of them positive:

> Hear the voice of my supplications, when I cry unto thee, when I lift up my hands toward thy holy oracle.

> Thus will I bless thee while I live: I will lift up my hands in thy name.

My hands also will I lift up unto thy commandments, which I have loved; and I will meditate in thy statutes.

Lift up your hands in the sanctuary, and bless the Lord.

Let my prayer be set forth before thee as incense; and the lifting up of my hands as the evening sacrifice.

Arise, cry out in the night; in the beginning of the watches pour out thine heart like water before the face of the Lord: lift up thy hands toward him for the life of thy young children, that faint for hunger in the top of every street.

Let us lift up our heart with our hands unto God in the heavens.

And Ezra blessed the Lord, the great God. And all the people answered, Amen, Amen, with lifting up their hands: and they bowed their heads, and worshiped the Lord with their faces to the ground.

I will therefore that men pray every where, lifting up holy hands, without wrath and doubting.[14]

Scriptural evidence on hand raising in worship is plenteous. Ellen White also refers positively to Solomon and Christ raising their hands to God as they prayed. In addition, she refers to herself doing so and even infers that she would be pleased if every ambassador for Christ would do so in pointing people to Jesus.[15] There can be no question that hand raising is a Biblical practice with wide support in Scripture and in the writings of Ellen White. To forbid people to raise hands in worship would be to take a stand against the Bible. This we must not do. To forbid that which God has commanded is extremely dangerous.

Hopefully this brief examination of worship expressions and musical styles will enable the reader to understand that there are varied tastes that need to be ministered to in worship. One size no longer fits all. We must allow for a wide expression of praise to God in our worship services. While some churches will not be comfortable with some of these forms, they must not stand in criticism of those who find such forms meaningful to their religious expression. Remember, in most cases the criticism is far worse than the object of the criticism.

Notes:

1. Ellen G. White, *Manuscript Releases*, vol. 3, 264.

2. Arthur White, *E. G. White Biography*, vol. 4, 446.

3. Ellen G. White, General Conference Bulletin, 4-14–03, "The Southern Work," pr. 6.

4. Arthur White, *E. G. White Biography*, vol. 1, 289.

5. Ellen G. White, Letter 31, 1876, quoted in *E. G. White Biography*, vol. 3, 39.

6. Ellen G. White, *Christian Service*, 164.

7. Discipleship training for cell churches is available through the North American Division Evangelism Institute in Berrien Springs, Michigan. The reader may also check the web site at *www.nadei.org*. Beginning training is available at the annual *Seeds* Church Planting Conferences. A basic book to read about the cell church would be Becham's *The Second Reformation*.

8. Ellen G. White, *The Voice in Speech and Song*, 434; idem., *Spirit of Prophecy*, vol 1, 28; idem., *Counsels on Health*, 481; idem., *Evangelism*, 500; Ibid., 503; idem., *Voice in Speech*, 434; idem., *Gospel Workers*, 357, 358.

9. Ellen G. White, *Gospel Workers*, 357.

10. Ellen G. White, *Review and Herald*, April 14, 1885.

11. Psalm 122:1.

12. Psalm 47:1.

13. Ellen G. White, quoted by Arthur White, *E. G. White Biography*, Vol. 3, 46.

14. Ps. 28:2; 63:4; 119:48; 134:2; 141:2; Lam. 2:29; 3:41; Neh. 8:6; 1 Tim. 2:8.

15. Ellen G. White, *Life Sketches of Ellen G. White* (Mountain View, Calif.: Pacific Press, 1915), 223; idem., *Signs of the Times*, Aug. 18, 1890.

9

Getting Started: The Prenatal Phase

So you're ready to begin planting a church! You feel called of God for this important, exciting task, you have decided on the kind of church God is calling you to plant (chapter 8), and you know how you will go about planting that church (chapter 7). Now it is time to begin the church planting process. What happens over the next several months will determine the success or failure of the new church.

In fact, you are still six to nine months away from having the first worship service in the new church. It would be easy to skip through the prenatal phase (the period before the first service occurs) and move to what is considered most important—getting the new church started. Yet experience has proven that the prenatal phase determines the success or failure of the church plant. This phase cannot be ignored or rushed through.

Location

Where are you going to plant the new church? It may be that you have no choice in the matter—the local conference may have called you to plant a new church in a specific location. In that case, your only input may be to choose the part of town in which the new church will be located. If you have not been told where to plant the church, then you must commence praying fervently that God will guide you in selecting the location. This is not mere form—one must seek divine guidance in this very important decision.

What are good locations for a new church? First of all, fast-growing areas are always good places to begin new work. Research has revealed that people who have recently moved to an area are more open and receptive to a change in religion (from no religion to a church, from a church to no religion, or from one denomination to another). Thus, communities that are seeing a large influx of people would be promising for a new church plant. However, when people seek out a church, they are usually seeking to build new relationships. Keeping this in mind, the church planter will conduct events that will enable people to begin building relationships in connection with the new church plant.

Another area where church planting can be successful is in highly receptive communities. Places where people are responding to the gospel indicate soil in which the Holy Spirit is currently preparing a harvest. We need to work where God is working. Look at other churches in the proposed area. Are they growing? Usually if conservative churches are expanding in an area, it is a place where Adventist churches will thrive also.

This does not mean that planters should ignore nonreceptive areas. It does mean, however, that these nonreceptive areas should not be prime targets for current church plants. These places may need to wait until God is moving in that area, preparing a harvest there. Only much time in prayer can enable the church planter to discover where God is at work. Success comes when the planter rides the waves of God's Spirit. As God prepares the ground, the planter moves in to sow the seed, cultivate, and then reap the harvest.

A third area for church planting is in densely populated communities. In large urban areas, millions of people live in close proximity. As we look over the metroplexes, we discover many areas with no Adventist presence. This absence may occur geographically or in people groups. Every metropolitan area in North America could easily double the number of churches without overchurching the area.

First, decide on geographical coverage. Take a map of the area, place a pin wherever there is currently an Adventist church. Now look at the map. What areas do not have pins? Look at the population of each area and then ask if one Adventist church can adequately minister to all the people in that area. Second, list all the people groups in that urban area: ethnic, cultural, and generational. Place a check mark beside each group that has an Adventist presence. What groups are being overlooked? Third, examine whether the church that is ministering to a certain group is located where that group resides. If not, a new church may be needed in another area of the metroplex.

These three simple steps do not involve a lot of work but will quickly reveal that most metropolitan areas are untouched by Adventist churches. And these three steps are not exhaustive. Much more detailed study can be done to examine carefully the places where new churches need to be planted. A new mindset needs to enter the Adventist thinking:

> Two churches are more complementary than competitive. Two churches minister to people of two different mind sets, two different cultural inclinations. They will reach nearly twice as many unchurched as one will.[1]

> In every city where the truth is proclaimed, churches are to be raised up. In some large cities there must be churches in various parts of the city.[2]

In understanding the place where God is calling you to plant a church, the wise planter will spend some time examining the demographics of the area. This is true even if the conference has already determined where the plant will be. It is very important to understand clearly the kinds of people who are residing in the target area. This information will enable the church planter to know how the community should be approached.

There are several sources for good demographic material. The easiest and cheapest is the local library, where you may examine the information from the latest census. This information will need interpretation. If the church planter does not have experience in examining demographic information, it would be important to employ an agency to examine and interpret the area for you. There is usually a small charge for this service, but it is generally well worth the expense. One of the best Adventist sources for demographic data is the Institute of Christian Ministry at Andrews University. They are able to evaluate the data and let the planter know what approach might best be used to begin Adventist work in that particular zip code.

A third source of information which should be consulted, even if one is using the other two methods, is the local Chamber of Commerce. They can tell you what part of town is expected to grow in the next few years, and also provide a lot of local information that would be unavailable elsewhere. Usually the information from the Chamber of Commerce is free.

Attracting the Nucleus

With the location settled and a basic understanding of the demographics of the area in mind, the church planter begins to attract a nucleus of people who will work with him/her over the next several months in preparation for beginning the new church. There are various ways to attract these people.

If the nucleus is to be formed from an existing Adventist church which is planning on being the mother of the new baby church, then most of the nucleus may have formed in the mother church. This would be forming a church through the "hiving off" method discussed in chapter seven. The danger here is that the new church is apt to be a clone of the mother church, since so many from the nucleus are coming from one church. If that is the desire, then it is fine to proceed. One caution as you gather the nucleus: Do not take so many people from the mother church that the mother is damaged. A figure that has proven reliable is 15 percent or less of the current attendance. In other words, if the mother church has an attendance of 100, you should not use more than 15 people out of that church. You might increase your nucleus by attracting people from several nearby Adventist churches.

Usually when a new plant starts, there is a slight dip in attendance and finances in the mother church for about six months. Then the church usually recovers and goes above where it was before the plant, both in attendance and in finances. However, if the planter takes more than 15 percent from the mother church, the recovery period will be longer, and some churches may never recover. This will create a backlash against church planting and will eventually harm both the mother church and all new plants.

If the vision for the church plant is for an entirely different paradigm, then it is important that there not be a large nucleus from other Adventist churches. In this case it is best to begin with a small nucleus of people committed to the new paradigm of church. In fact, entrance into the nucleus should be on the basis of complete agreement with the vision and plan for the new church. If people who are not committed to the vision join the nucleus, they will eventually kill the vision. In the desire to get the support of financial backers, the planter sometimes compromises the vision.

This is usually a fatal mistake that prevents the new church from reaching the harvest that God has planned for it.

Where, then, does the planter acquire the people for the nucleus? From the harvest! In fact, in mission-driven churches, beginning attendance usually consists of at least 50 percent who are recently or not yet gathered from the harvest. This gives a strong soul-winning bent to the new plant. When the nucleus of a church plant is composed almost entirely of existing members, the church rarely develops a harvest outlook; instead, it usually makes ministry to the saints its main focus. Harvest-centered churches are created out of the harvest. It is important that the nucleus include some existing Adventists committed to the new plant, but the larger the nucleus gleaned from the fields of labor, the higher the likelihood that this new Adventist church will continue to reap souls for the kingdom of God.

One source of members for the new harvest-centered church is former Adventists or Adventists not currently attending a local church. Ask nearby Adventist churches to share with you the names and addresses of members who are currently not attending. Visit them and seek to interest them in the new church plant. Many of them may be committed Adventists who have not related to the existing churches in the area but who may be open to becoming involved in the new church. One must use caution in selecting these people. Make certain that they are not trouble makers and are committed to the mission of the new church.

It is not necessary to have recruited the entire nucleus before you begin meeting together. As soon as possible, begin convening the nucleus and working through issues that need to be dealt with in preparation for the church plant. As others join the group, they can be brought up to date on issues that have already been discussed. In fact, only those Adventists should join who can agree with what has already been decided. New converts can easily be educated into the philosophy of the nucleus.

How large should be the nucleus before you have the first

worship service? That depends on the size you want the new church to be. If your plan is to plant a small church that is to remain small (fewer than 200 in worship), you can begin any time after the nucleus has worked through the issues to be discussed later in this chapter. However, if your desire is to plant a church that will grow to more than 200 in worship, you should not hold the first worship service until you would expect to have a minimum of 50 to 100 in attendance on Sabbath morning. The size of the nucleus for the first worship service is important. Large churches need to begin large. The lower the socio-economic status of the projected target, the nearer to 50 the nucleus can be. However, if you are planting in an area of high socio-economic status, it is important to be nearer to 100 for the first worship service.

In gathering the nucleus, the church planter already should have decided upon a target audience for the new church. Those who are recruited for the nucleus must understand that this church will be focused on reaching this specific target audience. In this new century, churches can no longer attempt to reach everyone; they must target certain groups. In recruiting the nucleus, it is imperative that several members of the target group be present in the nucleus. For example, if the focus of the church will be professional young adults, there must be several professional young adults in the nucleus. Others may be included in the nucleus, but unless a majority of the nucleus is composed of people from the target group it will not be successful in reaching them.

Creating Community in the Nucleus

The fact that people have gathered to plant a church and that they agree on its basic mission does not mean that they will automatically get along with each other. Various personalities will clash, and some people may not "fit" in the new church. It is imperative that the planter work diligently to build a real sense of community among the members of the nucleus. If this is not done during the prenatal phase, it will certainly not take place when the church is finally birthed. Some planters assume that community will be created eventually, and thus they proceed to establish a church with a group of people who are not living in biblical community. This is a sad mistake.

One of the first steps is to help these people in the nucleus learn to *love* each other. While love is inherent in one who has come to Christ, expressing that love is usually a learned activity. Seminars like *Learning to Love* from **Concerned Communications** do an excellent job of helping a group begin the learning process of expressing Christ's love among themselves and to the community they will eventually serve. If love is not formed during this nucleus-building phase, the likelihood of the new church being a loving community of faith is greatly diminished.

The second area on which church planters must focus with the nucleus is *prayer*. The group needs to learn to pray together and to spend a considerable portion of their time together in prayer for themselves, for the harvest, and for the new church plant. New churches must be bathed in prayer. Later on we will devote an entire chapter to this important topic.

The third area for focus is *faith*. Church planters must help the nucleus see what God can do. They must capture God's vision for the harvest. Sharing stories of God's leading as the nucleus begins to reach out into the community will help build this dynamic. They must clearly see that God is working through them to reach the harvest, and they must have faith that God will be able to do great things through this new church plant. The faith dynamic will solidify the group for the accomplishment of their mission in the power of God.

The fourth area of focus is *purpose*. While there has been some initial agreement on the purpose of the new church before people joined the nucleus, it is now time to bring strong cohesion to that purpose. There must be no question among those who have formed the nucleus that God has called them together for the purpose of planting a church. And there should be basic agreement on what the new church will look like once it gets planted. Much of this purpose will be discovered as the group seeks to uncover its *core values*, which will be discussed in the next section.

A fifth area of focus for church planters is *agreement on a philosophy of ministry*. In earlier chapters we explored the issue of creating non-pastor-dependent churches that enable lay ministry. This concept must be explored and agreement reached before the new church opens. If the expectation of the nucleus is that the pastor will be the chaplain instead of the trainer, very little of the harvest will be reaped from this church, and it will mainly attract existing Adventists from other churches who want a maintenance ministry. It is much easier to set up a church on the basis of lay ministry than to transition an existing church from pastor dependency to lay empowerment.

During the time that the nucleus meets together, it would be well for the group to spend some time reading and studying the author's trilogy on lay ministry: *Revolution in the Church*, *Radical Disciples for Revolutionary Churches*, and *The Revolutionized Church of the 21ˢᵗ Century*.[3] The group should not simply read through these books, but take time to discuss each chapter and ask how these principles can be incorporated into the new church that they are planting.

The purpose for discussing the five focus points mentioned above is not only to create unity among the nucleus, but also to enable them to think through ways in which they can incorporate each of these dynamics into the new church plant. The purpose is not merely to unite the nucleus, but to help them formulate plans by which all who join the church will become fully devoted in the same way. So first, planters must labor to create unity among the group. Once that has been accomplished, they can move on to establishing the idea into the fabric of the new church plant.

Core Values

Core values refer to those defining values that will characterize the new church. Agreement on the core values is absolutely essential for the new church. Most conflicts within churches occur over core values. These are not the same as doctrines. We have deliberately not discussed doctrines for the new church because it is assumed that any Adventist church plant will be in complete agreement with the twenty-seven fundamental beliefs of the Adventist church. Why would anyone want to plant an Adventist church if they didn't believe the basic doctrines of the church? The author makes this statement with "tongue in cheek," because this has become a problem in some quarters. However, for the purposes of this book, agreement with the doctrines will be assumed.

Another assumption of this book is that new church plants will support the organizational structure of the Adventist Church. The plan of remitting the entire tithe to the conference is not up for grabs in Adventism at this time. This is a not a doctrine, but clearly it is a core value of the Adventist Church. Those planting Adventist churches must therefore be in harmony with that basic organizational plan; otherwise they should not attempt to plant an Adventist church. Adventism has plenty of room for divergence in how people "do" church, but it has little room for those who are not supportive of the basic structure that has made the Adventist Church a strong world movement. This would include a willingness to submit to the counsel and guidance of the local conference which has credentialed the church planter.

However, in people's minds core values are very close to doctrines. In fact, many have elevated a core value to the point of doctrine, making it extremely difficult to tolerate people whose core values differ. It is highly important for the nucleus to discuss their core values and to agree on them. It would be well for the nucleus to list those core values in writing so that anyone, especially transferring Adventists, could see them and clearly understand that agreement with them was essential in order to join the new church.

Different churches will have different core values. There are not universal core values for all Adventist churches to simply adopt. Of course, it would be wise for the Adventist Church as a whole to adopt some very basic core values for the entire denomination, such as tithe distribution. However, these should be very minimal, and then churches should be allowed to develop provided they agree with the twenty-seven fundamental beliefs and the core values of the denomination.

In this section we desire to focus on the core values of a local church, and these will be different with each church. Let me suggest some areas for discussion among the nucleus concerning core values, remembering that various churches may approach each of these in a different way, but that the nucleus must decide on them during the prenatal phase.

A very basic core value is a passion to reach lost people. One would expect every church to embrace this value. However, reality indicates that in most churches this is not a defining value. This value does not say simply that there are some means within the church for reaching lost people—it goes to the very core of the church. It states in unequivocal terms that reaching lost people is the central focus of this church. Only when there is a tremendous compassion to reach lost people will the new church be harvest centered. The great need in Adventist church planting today is that this core value have center stage. This would mean that everything the church does would be evaluated by how well it reaches the harvest. This type of church does not exist to focus on the saved, but on the great harvest that God is calling it to reach. The plans, programs, and activities of a church with this core value are always harvest centered rather than member centered.

A second core value that the nucleus will need to discuss extensively is a culturally relevant style. Once the nucleus has decided on the target group for the new church, it is imperative that the church utilize a style that is culturally relevant to them. The needs of the unchurched target groups determine our programs, their hang-ups determine our strategy, their culture determines our style, and their population determines our goals. If we focus on the lost, our style must be compatible with the mindset of the lost. This does not mean compromising the message to reach the lost, but that it is packaged in the language of your target group.

To fail to present the message in a culturally relevant style is like planting a Chinese-speaking church in Denver, Colorado, and insisting that anyone in Denver who wished to become an Adventist learn Chinese. That seems ridiculous, but that is precisely what we do when we fail to use a culturally relevant style. Remember that music is also a language.

Much serious discussion is needed about the above-mentioned core value. If there is not agreement here during the prenatal phase, there will be a continual undercurrent that will eventually destroy the new church. The nucleus should spend as much time as needed on this core value until consensus is reached. If any part of the nucleus does not agree here, the church will not succeed. Any Adventist who joins the group in the future also must be in agreement with this core value. Those who join from the harvest obviously will be in agreement with the core value, otherwise they would not have been attracted to the church. However, that core value needs to be clearly articulated to new converts. It must never be assumed.

A third core value is a Great Commission consciousness. This needs to be inbred in the church from the very beginning. When a Great Commission core value takes possession of the church, they will see the potential harvest.

A fourth core value that will need much discussion is a philosophy of lay development. This means that the church focuses on developing leaders and releasing them for ministry. A comprehensive training program for new people will need to be developed. Not only will lay people need training, but they must be released for ministry. One of the most difficult assignments for most churches is to release people for actual ministry. Most churches are structured to keep ministry from happening. From the very beginning the church structure will need to be streamlined so that most of its people are free for ministry involvement instead of being tied up on committees. It also means that church boards should see their function as giving permission for ministry to actually occur, rather than to keep ministries from beginning.

A final core value that is vitally important to implant in the church during the prenatal phase is that it must plant other churches. If reproduction is not implanted in the "DNA" of the church from the very beginning, it probably will not happen regularly. In fact, some have suggested that a new church plant should plant another church within the first 36-48 months of its existence, otherwise this concept will never be impregnated into their "DNA." The great fear of new churches is that they will lose resources too quickly. However, the church must be continually reminded that the resources are always in the harvest. As they reach out and find people in the harvest, they can release them back into the harvest for yet another harvest. There is simply no limit to the expansion of the church when it accepts the fact that it is a reproduction organization.

Other core values will need discussion. Each church will need to work through them. However, the core values mentioned above can be a beginning step in developing some basic core values among the nucleus. If these core values are to be part of the genetic code of the church, they must be implanted during the prenatal phase. Once the issues brought to light in this chapter have been dealt with and the nucleus is large enough to begin the first service, the new church is ready to begin. Chapter 11 will examine the first year in the life of the new church, but first we will examine the role of prayer as a means to begin to gather the harvest.

Notes:

1. M. Wendell Belew, *Church Growth: America*, vol. 2, no. 5, 7.

2. Ellen G. White, *Medical Ministry,* 309.

3. These books are available through your local Adventist Book Center.

10

The Spiritual Dynamic in Church Planting

Church planting is a spiritual battle. Those who engage in it are on the front lines of ministry and are therefore the subject of Satan's special attacks. Church planters more than almost any other Christian workers face the onslaught of the enemy. Church planters are robbing Satan of his territory, and he will not give up without a struggle. That's why most church planters will report that the most essential need of church planters is prayer. Those working in the front lines of ministry quickly sense their need of dependence upon God.

Paul, that aggressive church planter, understood this battle. There was no question in his mind that he was engaged in spiritual warfare:

> Put on the armor that God gives, so you can defend yourself against the devil's tricks. We are not fighting against humans. We are fighting against forces and authorities and against rulers of dark-

ness and powers in the spiritual world. So put on all the armor that God gives. Then when that evil day comes, you will be able to defend yourself. And when the battle is over, you will still be standing firm.[1]

There is perhaps no activity of the church that enrages the devil more than church planting. That's why it is so critical that church planters spend a significant amount of time in prayer and have plenty of prayer support as they move into church planting. Satan does not relinquish his territory without a struggle. Our power is not in technique or methodology; our strength is in our dependence upon God.

Prayer Partners

As church planters commence, one of their first steps should be to secure several individuals who will be their personal intercessors. These should not be people who pray only occasionally for the church planters, but who will enter into an all-out prayer vigil for them. Each church planter should have at least two or three people who have covenanted to be prayer partners. These prayer partners should have the gift of intercession and agree to spend a specific amount of time every day praying for the church planter.

Being a prayer partner with a church planter is a two-way street. In order for the prayer partners to pray effectively, they must be kept informed regularly by the church planter about what is happening in the church plant. The intercessor needs to be able to pray specifically. Sometimes church planters simply ask someone to pray, but fail to maintain communication with them. That will not be sufficient for the spiritual battle being waged. Therefore, it is of utmost importance to be in contact at least weekly, and more often when there are crises. The intercessor does not have to be part of the nucleus or even live near the plant. Modern communication means that intercessors anywhere can pray for the church planter.

There should be a minimum of three prayer intercessors for each church planter on the team. At least one of these should be a part of the nucleus. In addition to personal intercessors, church planters need as many individuals as possible, including the entire nucleus, to pray regularly for the church plant. However, the intercession of these will not be as intense as that of the personal intercessors. Prayer must bathe all activities of the church planting process.

The Power of Prayer

Never underestimate the power of prayer. This is the secret of successful church plants. Methodology is important—the right steps should be taken in the church planting process—but unless those engaged in the church planting process are bathed in prayer, nothing significant will happen. That's why it is extremely important that the members of the nucleus take significant time each week to pray together. As they work through their core values, the nucleus will many times reach an impasse in their discussions. There will be many disagreements as they seek the harmony of the Spirit. At such times, the members of the nucleus must get down on their knees, as did the early pioneers of Adventism in a similar situation over doctrine, and ask God to guide them to the right core values. Every decision of the nucleus must be bathed in prayer.

Praying together will result in a spirit of revival taking possession of the group. Just as the early church was brought into one accord as they spent significant time praying together, so the nucleus will be drawn together as they pray through their problems. Bob Logan defines revival this way:

> Revival is an outpouring of the Holy Spirit in great power in such a way that people are aware of God's holiness and love in a way they have never known before, resulting in bold witness and service to advance the kingdom of God.[2]

Revival is not just warm fuzzy feelings. Genuine revival always results in people being won to Jesus. If the revival only keeps the church in the church it is not a genuine movement of the Spirit. Genuine revival sends the church out of the pews and into the streets. There is a greater concern for God's holiness, so the standard of God is uplifted, but coupled with that increased worship of God is the fervent passion for the lost that now develops in response to the revival fires of the Holy Spirit moving upon the church. Revival fires will send the church to its knees:

> The time has come for a thorough reformation to take place. When reformation begins, the spirit of prayer will actuate every believer, and will banish from the church the spirit of discord and strife.[3]

Yet it doesn't take a large group of people to bring about this kind of prayer revival in a group of believers. "When churches are revived, it is because some individual seeks for the blessing of God." "I saw that one saint if he were right could move the arm of God."[4]

Prayer brings revival, and revival brings more prayer. Church planters must move aggressively forward as they plant new churches, but they must move forward on their knees. A church on its knees is a church on the threshold of receiving power. What will happen among the nucleus as they spend significant time in prayer for a revival spirit? Listen to Ellen White as she describes what happens when the Holy Spirit descends upon a group of believers:

> The baptism of the Holy Ghost on the day of Pentecost will lead to a revival of true religion, and to the performance of many wonderful works.. Heavenly intelligences will come among us, and men will speak as they are moved upon by the Holy Spirit of God. But should the Lord work upon men as he did on, and after the day of Pentecost, many who now claim to believe the truth, would know so very little of the operation of the Holy Spirit, that they would cry, "Beware of fanaticism." They would say of those who were filled with the Spirit, "These men are drunk with new wine."...the great

sin of those who profess to be Christians is that they do not open the heart to receive the Holy Spirit. When souls long after Christ, and seek to become one with him, then those who are content with the form of godliness, exclaim "Be careful, do not go to extremes." When the angels of heaven come among us, and work through human agents, there will be solid, substantial conversions, after the order of the conversions after the day of Pentecost. Now brethren, be careful not to go into human excitement, we should not be among those who will raise inquires, and cherish doubts in reference to the work of the "Spirit of God; for there will be those who will question and criticize when the Spirit of God takes possession of men and women, because their own hearts are not moved; but are cold and unimpressible."[5]

When the Holy Spirit works the human agent, it does not ask us in what way it shall operate. Often it moves in unexpected ways.[6]

Church planters must not be afraid of the Holy Spirit descending upon them. Indeed, "strange things" might happen, unexpected ideas will come to their minds, but the ideas will have been impressed upon them by the Holy Spirit. The result will be seen in that many precious souls will come to know Jesus.

As the nucleus begins to pray together, unity will form and a great burden for the lost will develop in their hearts. As they continue to pray, their prayers will be directed from harmony within to the lost without. The members of the nucleus ought to be able to identify several people who are possible candidates for the new church. These people now become the object of their prayers. Separately and especially at every meeting of the nucleus, these names are presented before the Lord, asking the Holy Spirit to open their hearts to the gospel as the members of the nucleus seek to reach them.

Jesus asked us to pray powerfully for lost people. We do not have to pray that lost people be found "if it is in accordance with God's will." God has already told us that it is His will that the lost be found. We can pray with full assurance that God will speak to the these people, and unless they stubbornly resist the promptings of the Holy Spirit, they will yield to God's drawing power. The nucleus should choose Matthew 18:19 as one of their promise texts and hold it before the Lord regarding each person on their prayer list: "I promise that when any two of you on earth agree about something you are praying for, my Father in heaven will do it for you."[7]

We are talking here of praying with strong faith, claiming the promise of God to perform what we ask regarding the salvation of those whom we have identified as possible candidates for the kingdom of God. Ellen White tells of a similar incident in the early days of the Millerite movement:

> I arranged meetings with my young friends, some of whom were considerably older than myself, and a few were married persons. A number of them were vain and thoughtless; my experience sounded to them like an idle tale, and they did not heed my entreaties. But I determined that my efforts should never cease till these dear souls, for whom I had so great an interest, yielded to God. Several entire nights were spent by me in earnest prayer for those whom I had sought out and brought together for the purpose of laboring and praying with them.

> Some of these had met with us from curiosity to hear what I had to say; others thought me beside myself to be so persistent in my efforts, especially when they manifested no concern on their own part. But at every one of our little meetings I continued to exhort and pray for each one separately, until every one had yielded to Jesus, acknowledging the merits of His pardoning love. Every one was converted to God.[8]

Here was the beginning of Adventism. Notice how people were won: through prayer and prayer alone. Ellen White literally prayed people into Jesus. Notice that this was not casual prayer, but heartfelt, earnest supplication to God for the salvation of specific souls. It is this kind of intensity that needs to take possession of the nucleus planning for the new church. Let the burden of souls consume them as they literally pray people into the kingdom of God. Not only did Ellen White practice this kind of fervent prayer in her own spiritual life, she advocated that the church develop this same kind of intense earnestness for lost people:

> Souls are to be sought for, prayed for, labored for. Earnest appeals are to be made. Fervent prayers are to be offered. Our tame, spiritless petitions are to be changed into petitions of intense earnestness. God's word declares: "the effectual fervent prayer of a righteous man availeth much."[9]

> Why do not believers feel a deeper, more earnest concern for those who are out of Christ? Why do not two or three meet together and plead with God for the salvation of some special one, and then for still another?[10]

> Let the workers grasp the promises of God saying: "Thou hast promised, 'Ask, and ye shall receive.' I must have this soul converted to Jesus Christ." Solicit prayer for the souls for whom you labor; present them before the church as objects for their supplication. It will be just what the church needs, to have their minds called from their little petty difficulties, to feel a great burden, a personal interest, for a soul that is ready to perish. Select another and still another soul, daily seeking guidance from God, laying everything before Him in earnest prayer, and working in divine wisdom. As you do this, you will see that God will give the Holy Spirit to convict; and the power of the truth to convert the soul.[11]

There is no mistaking the counsel of Ellen White. People are reached by prayer, and churches are started by intense, earnest prayer. This kind of prayer needs to occupy a considerable amount of time as the nucleus begins to focus on the lost through prayer. However, praying alone is not sufficient. Those who are praying must get up off their knees and contact the lost. The story is told of a group of believers who were praying for the town's mayor. After praying for some time, one of those kneeling suddenly got up off his knees and made the suggestion that one of them ought to contact the mayor and invite him to come to Christ. Action must proceed from the prayers of the nucleus.

Prayer for the Community

During the nucleus-building phase, the core members will need to begin reaching out into the community. However, this reaching out must be bathed in prayer. Door-to-door work has become increasingly difficult in this age. Most people are resistant to religious people coming to the door to "sell" their religion. A prayer strategy can still make door-to-door work effective in the twenty-first century.[12]

The church planter should divide the church planting territory into city blocks. Each member of the nucleus should then choose one or two blocks as his or her special prayer territory. Having chosen a block, the nucleus member then goes to the territory and walks up and down the street, praying for each home. No contact is made at the door at this time. Individuals are silently praying for each home as they walk the block. However, needs will start becoming apparent as the person observes the community. For example, toys in the yard will indicate a young family with children; a handicap ramp may indicate a person with a wheelchair. This will enable the person to begin to make their prayers more meaningful.

Having done prayer walks for several weeks, the individual is now ready for the second phase of the community prayer program. This time, instead of simply walking the blocks and praying, the individual should knock on the door. The visitor tells the neighbor that they are from a new Adventist church beginning in the neighborhood. They are seeking to get better acquainted with their new neighbors by praying for them. Then ask for specific prayer requests. Most visitors will find a positive response to this approach, and many people will share their prayer requests.

The nice thing about this approach is that the visitors are not trying to get people to join their church or asking them for money. They are simply there to pray for the people. People really appreciate this approach. If some of the members of the nucleus are hesitant to knock on the doors, they can leave a door hanger that says they are praying for the people and asking for prayer requests, and then pick them up later.[13] This approach will not generate as many responses as knocking on the doors, but it does enable the shy members of the nucleus to be involved in the project.

Having secured the prayer requests, the visitor should pray in earnest for these requests, not only privately, but also in the meetings of the nucleus. After praying for a couple of weeks, the visitor should go back to the home, tell the person that they have been praying for them and their requests, and ask how it is going. They will discover that many answers to prayer have already occurred. At this point, the visitor can either offer to continue to pray for them or ask if there are other requests that they can pray about. If appropriate, the visitor might even suggest praying right at the door for the needs of the home. The visitor should go back to each home every couple of weeks, repeating the above scenario. It will take six to eight return visits to build enough confidence to move to the next level.

After building confidence through six to eight weeks of praying for people, the occupant will recognize the visitor immediately and will smile and quickly offer their prayer needs without the visitor even asking. By this time, the occupant probably will have invited the visitor inside and conversation will have moved to items other than the prayer requests, although the prayer requests should always remain in the forefront. Other conversation enables the visitor to begin to develop a friendship and relationship with the occupant of the home.

Once a relationship has been built, the visitor may mention that there is a group of people in the neighborhood who meet regularly to pray for each other. If appropriate, the visitor may extend an invitation for the person to join this prayer group. The group probably will consist of some of the members of the nucleus and some of the neighbors who have been prayed for. The prayer visitor should make certain that the group meets in the neighborhood where the person lives who is being invited. The group should be centered on prayer. There may be a Bible study on prayer or study of a book about praying more effectively, but it should be a prayer group.

Many of the people who have responded to the prayer walks will eventually join a prayer group. As they meet with the group week after week, deeper bonds will form, and many of the attendees from the prayer walks will begin to move into Bible studies. They will be key individuals to invite to the first worship service at the new church.

This chapter has focused on prayer in the context of starting a new church. Much of this counsel would be appropriate for an existing church, but it is *imperative* for new church plants. The prayer strategy suggested in this chapter is designed to help the church develop "mission eyes" even before the church begins. Prayer is not something done only in the bounds of the church; prayer must be an activity of the church as it interacts with the surrounding community.

The secret of success in church planting revolves heavily around the ability of church planters to help the nucleus begin to pray for each other, for people they know, and for the people of the community that they do not know. God will bless with tangible results as these people who have been the objects of prayer move into the worshiping community. Church planters must make certain that their new church is a praying church by incorporating the prayer strategy from the very beginning, even during the prenatal phase.

Notes:

1. Ephesians 6:11-13 (Contemporary English Version).

2. Dr. Robert Logan, *Church Planting Syllabus*, Fuller Seminary, 1996.

3. Ellen G. White, *Testimonies*, vol. 8, 251.

4. Ellen G. White, *Christian Service*, 121; idem, *Early Writings*, 120.

5. Ellen G. White, *1888 Materials*, 1250, 1251.

6. Ibid., 1540.

7. Matthew 18:19 (Contemporary English Version).

8. Ellen G. White, *Life Sketches*, 41, 42.

9. Ellen G. White, *Testimonies*, vol. 7, 12.

10. Ibid., 21.

11. Ellen G. White, *Medical Ministry*, 244, 245.

12. The initial idea for this prayer strategy was spawned through the reading of Ed Silvoso's book, *That None Should Perish* (Ventura, Calif.: Regal, 1994).

13. Door hangers for this project are available from Seminars Unlimited (1-800-982-3344).

11

The First Year of the New Church

The prenatal period is over. It is time to birth the new baby. Your nucleus group has worked through all the issues discussed in chapter 9, they have been praying intensely for the new church, and you feel the group should number between 100-200 at your first worship service. So you are ready to begin. Don't hold the first service, however, until you are ready for this step. Once you hold the first service, the expectations of those involved are much higher. If the church does not come together as expected at this point, it may be very difficult to turn things around. However, don't wait too long to begin or your nucleus group is apt to get discouraged.

Getting the Nucleus to 50-100

You've worked through the issues with the nucleus, but you still need to get the group up to 50-100. You don't want to flood the group with Adventists who have not bought into the focus of the new church. How can your small nucleus build up to the 50-100 range needed to start a major church?

In the Adventist setting this is best done through a small group approach.

One of the books that many in the nucleus may have read already, or the group may have studied together, is the author's book *The Revolutionized Church of the 21ˢᵗ Century*. In this book we explore the idea of biblical community and using a small group approach to solidify existing Adventists and to reach out to new people. When starting a cell church, this approach is absolutely vital, but those starting other churches also will find the small group approach an excellent way to increase the nucleus.

Begin the small groups with your nucleus members. Your nucleus may have been acting much like a small group already, but it will be important, first of all, to train leaders for the groups. Many small group training materials are available. If you need help in this area, contact NADEI at (616) 471-9220. For illustration purposes, let's suppose your nucleus now numbers twenty to twenty-five adults. You've settled on the core values with this group and are ready to expand your nucleus as you get ready for the first service.

With twenty to twenty-five adults, and assuming your nucleus is totally committed to this approach, you should train leaders for three to four groups. Each group will need a leader, an assistant leader, and a host. The members of the nucleus then choose one of the three groups to join, which should place seven or eight people in each group, including the leaders. Each person in the group then works at bringing friends, neighbors, and other interests to the group meetings, so the groups start expanding to twelve to fifteen.

Once the groups achieve twelve to fifteen in attendance, they should plan to multiply by beginning a new group. The assistant leader now becomes the leader. At the same time, two new assistant leaders are chosen to be trained: one for the existing group, and an assistant leader for the new group. Never should a group begin without a leader and an assistant leader in place.

Keep expanding the groups until there are fifty to a hundred people in attendance at the groups. Not all of them may become part of the new church, but many of them will. If you have fifty to one hundred in the groups, you have an excellent possibility of having the requisite number of people for your first worship service. This is a simple way to expand the nucleus slowly without worrying about being a church and carrying all the excess baggage entailed in attempting to provide the services of a church.

The important thing here is to make certain that adequate leadership development is occurring. The small groups can multiply only as trained leadership becomes available. The church planter will therefore spend considerable time training the members of the nucleus to serve as group leaders and making certain that the groups are continually reaching out to nonmembers and inviting them to the groups, then multiplying the group as soon as possible with the new leadership.

Even if the church plant is not a cell church, this multiplication of groups must continue, especially throughout the first year. It will be one of the best tools to continually expand the church during those critical first months. If evangelism is not rooted and grounded in the church during this first year, the new church will probably never be a soul-winning church. Since church planting focuses on the lost, it is vital that evangelism be incorporated into the groups from the beginning; otherwise, they will be nurture groups and will hinder the church from growing instead of helping it.

Evangelism During the First Year

During the time that the church planter is building up the nucleus, and throughout the first year, it is highly important to focus on a strong evangelistic plan. This will help not only in building up the nucleus, but also in expanding the nucleus during the critical first year of existence. Sometimes the nucleus is so foreign to the community where the plant is to be made that there are few if any contacts in the community. In that case, the planter will need to assist the people in building contacts. One of the ways to do this is through felt-need ministries. These ministries enable the nucleus members to reach out and begin to make contacts in the community, and they also create good will and a good name for the new church being planned.

If each small group will sponsor a felt-need ministry, then in the above scenario there could be three ministries beginning during the nucleus-building phase. This should provide the new church with many significant contacts which could eventually provide new members for the groups as well as for the new church.

A felt-need event is a program, plan, or ministry that focuses on contacting unreached people in the target community. The plan should focus on the felt needs of the people in the target group. For example, if the target group is Gen-Xers, ministries that focus on building relationships would be appropriate, because it is known that Gen-Xers are starving for meaningful relationships. If the target includes people who have experienced divorce, a divorce recovery seminar and follow-up group might be a good ministry to choose. Your nucleus should contain people who have similar needs to the target group if you are going to be successful in bridging the gap to reach them.

Conducting felt-need events is not limited to simply holding a seminar on a particular topic. The seminar is important, but the seminar must be followed up with a long-term support group. Here, relationships will be built that will enable the members to share Jesus with these people at the appropriate time. For example, suppose that one small group in the nucleus decides to focus on helping divorced people. A divorce recovery seminar is conducted. The seminars are not conducted solely for the community people who come, but the small group members intermingle with them as full participants. During the seminar, significant relationships will be formed. At the end of the seminar, the participants are invited to an ongoing divorce recovery group that will meet once a week, and many of the participants, because of the relationships which have been formed, will gladly join the ongoing group. The group meeting may be the regular meeting of the small group, but it now focuses on divorce recovery with a Christian emphasis. This emphasis has been articulated clearly to the people before they join the group. As people attend and hear Christian answers to the relational problem of divorce, their curiosity about Christianity will be piqued. Questions will be asked, Bible studies will be started, and many will be led to Jesus.

Other more traditional evangelistic approaches may be used during this time, such as Bible studies started through an invitational mailing. The focus of the nucleus should be on evangelism, especially throughout this first year. Over the next several months, acquaintances will be made and interests will be cultivated. However, it is not sufficient simply to cultivate the interest—a clear plan for reaping the interest must be inaugurated. Adventism requires a little different approach from what other evangelical churches do to start a church and reap the interest.

While other churches will simply invite the people to church at this point and work on assimilation, Adventism has a message to share before people can be brought into church membership. This never can be neglected. People simply do not appear on Sabbath morning as a result of utilizing the methods shared above. While this approach may work for people who have a previous background in Adventism, it will not succeed with people whose religious background does not include Sabbath worship. Therefore, in order to reap the cultivated interests into a new Adventist church, a definite plan for reaping those interests must be inaugurated.

The traditional Adventist method of reaping has been a public evangelistic event. The tragedy is that many churches have relied on the meeting to accomplish sowing, cultivating, and reaping, instead of using it properly as a reaping tool only. In response to this misuse, some have attempted to throw out public evangelism completely and use methodologies more common in traditional evangelical churches. However, as noted, in most cases this has not worked for Adventists. Instead, Adventist churches need to do all that has been suggested, and add the reaping part of the process. Evangelism is a process, and reaping is a part of that process. If reaping is not included, there will be little success.

A public evangelistic meeting as part of the reaping process can take different forms. Some churches will desire to run a full-blown crusade, others may choose to conduct a Prophecy Seminar, and some may settle for a class that teaches the message and invites people to become a part of the church as a result. The public evangelistic event, however conducted, has been and will continue to be a viable tool for beginning new congregations.

The First Worship Service

The first step in planning for the opening service is to find a location. Adventists meeting on Sabbath have far more options available than do most Sunday-keeping churches. Many churches of other denominations are willing to rent their facilities to Adventists. However, this goes both ways—Adventists should be willing to rent their facilities to other groups as well. This is just plain Christian courtesy.

If the nucleus group decides that they wish to begin worship services in a church building, they should choose a facility conducive to the style of worship that the new church will seek to conduct. For example, if the new church has chosen to use an informal service with a lot of participation from the congregation, it would not be conducive to rent an Episcopalian or Lutheran church that is structured for a highly liturgical service. Likewise, if your new church is planning on using a more liturgical service, you would not want to rent a Pentecostal-style church. Choose the building that best reflects the worship emphasis your new church desires to implement.

Another factor in the choice of the building is the size of the sanctuary. Do not choose a large sanctuary in which the congregation will feel lost. Try to find a church with a seating capacity that your group will at least half fill on the first Sabbath. Likewise, do not choose a sanctuary with such a small seating capacity that the congregation will outgrow it very quickly. Attendance on the first Sabbath will probably be larger than normal—up to twice as large as that which will be sustained on a regular basis—simply because of the newness. That is why it is important to have fifty to one hundred in the nucleus before holding the first worship service. Any people who stay by who were not in the nucleus add to that number. However, some Adventist churches that are being intentionally harvest centered are not allowing Adventists to join unless they go through an orientation class and agree with the direction of the church.

Depending upon the situation, it might be best to not meet in a church for the first worship service. Churches that are attracting the younger, more visual generation actually discover they have a better response if they choose an auditorium for the first meeting place. If that is the direction the church planter wishes to pursue, a local school auditorium would be a possible site. They usually have classrooms that would be available for Sabbath School. Other possibilities would be theaters or public auditoriums. In choosing a location, discover the reputation of the auditorium or church under consideration for rental. That reputation will affect the way in which people will view your church.

There are certain times in the year when it might be easier to begin a church. Many Sunday churches, for example, attempt to begin their new church around Christmas or Easter, when more people think about going to church. However, that does not necessarily work for Adventist churches. One good time to begin is in the fall, when the children are beginning a new school year, especially if you are centered on reaching families with young children.

One avenue that has helped a lot of Adventist churches begin with a good attendance is to commence services during a Prophecy Seminar or public evangelistic meeting. After the Sabbath has been presented, the attendees are invited to the church service for the next Sabbath as a regular part of the evangelistic series. This becomes the first Sabbath for the new church. This plan actually has been the most successful way of beginning an Adventist church. In this scenario, the first few weeks are totally evangelistic, which helps set an evangelistic tone for the life of the church.

Whenever the new service begins, it should be carefully planned and be done well. It should be an exciting service that centers on the visitors who will be attending. Most first-time attendees will be making the decision to return based on what they experience in that first worship service. Therefore, practice the service ahead of time. Rent the facility for one or two weeks in advance of the first service. During those weeks, the people in the nucleus should have a worship service there, so that they become familiar with the facility and the service. It will be helpful for the children's Sabbath School leaders to become familiar with their rooms and some of the children who will be coming. Then everyone can focus on visitors during the opening worship service, the whole service will run smoothly, and the visitors will see a well-polished service.

While the focus is on the visitors for the first week, that does not mean that they should be singled out. Don't ask the visitors to stand and introduce themselves. That is very awkward for most unchurched visitors and will prevent many of them from returning. Each member should do his or her best to help the guests feel welcome, and the church will need to find an inconspicuous way of letting the visitors obtain more information about the church and leave their name and address for future contact. A welcome table in the foyer could provide this service.

Once the names and addresses are obtained, the visitors should be contacted within forty-eight hours. It is best if this contact is made by a lay person and probably is best done by telephone rather than personal visit. The purpose of the visit is to let the visitor know that the church appreciated their visit, to ask if they have any questions about the church, and to encourage them to return. When the visitors return the second time, a home visit should be scheduled, Bible studies might be started, or the people might be invited to participate in one of the groups of the church. Make certain that visitors are carefully followed up and not allowed to "slip through the cracks."

Keeping the Church Growing

Because of their heavy concentration on evangelism during the prenatal phase, the nucleus group might feel that they have accomplished their basic evangelistic purpose and now must concentrate on building the church with the people they have already gathered. Nothing could be further from the truth! If the new church plant is to be harvest centered, then evangelism must be woven into every fiber of the church during this first year. The church must continue the multiplication of small groups with felt-need events and plan for another reaping event. Since the new church does not yet have facilities in which to invest, the church can invest in something far more precious than bricks and mortar: people!

In order for the new group to continue to grow, several important steps will need to be taken during the first year. Make certain that the small groups continue to expand and grow. If a church is to move beyond an attendance of two hundred, continual expansion of the fellowship groups is probably the most important step. Never should a group begin without a leader and an apprentice leader in place and a goal to multiply the group within six months to a year. If this is to be a reality, the church will need to invest heavily in training new leaders for all the groups. The continued growth of the church during the first year and into the future will be determined by the number of apprentice leaders the church can adequately train. Leadership training must not be limited to Adventists who were part of the nucleus. People with leadership qualities should be identified among the new converts and trained to be small group leaders. Only thus will the growth cycle continue.

It is also essential that the planter establish the new church on the model of leadership known as the trainer/equipper. If the planter starts the church as a shepherd or chaplain and the new church immediately develops a pastor dependency, it will be nearly impossible to move the church out of that model and into the trainer/equipper model. So the new church must be established in the model of leadership that the church planter desires to see continued. Even if this is a lay church plant, it is very easy to develop a pastor dependency. In this case the lay person simply assumes the position of the pastor, and the people depend on the lay person in the same way that they would depend on a pastor. This is not a lay church, but a lay-pastor-dependent church. In a true lay church, leadership is shared and the equipper model is fully utilized.

A third area of concern in the developing church during its first year is the mobilization of members for ministry as soon as they join the fledgling church. In fact, some new Adventist churches are making involvement in ministry a requirement for membership. This creates a much higher commitment level in the church, and perhaps it is time to raise the standard of membership in Adventist churches to include involvement in ministry as the expected norm of church membership.

Churches placing new people into ministry will need to regularly conduct spiritual gifts seminars and inaugurate the Lay Ministry Committee to place people into ministry in harmony with their spiritual gifts. In fact, one of the issues which the new church will need to grapple with is whether to inaugurate the traditional Nominating Committee process or begin the plant in the Lay Ministry mode by placing people into ministry in harmony with their giftedness rather than nominating everyone for office.[1] It is best to start the church in this mode rather than beginning in the traditional mode and then attempting to transition to the Lay Ministry process.

Having a Lay Ministry Committee does not mean that there will be no Nominating Committee. Some have attempted to go to extremes here and totally eliminate the Nominating Committee. If this is done, there is no one who can be held accountable. Our plea is to not nominate people into ministries, but *church officers* will need to be elected in order to be held accountable. Each church will need to decide which offices will be filled by election. A minimum would be the church board. The present problem is created by attempting to elect all positions, right down to the pianist for Cradle Roll Sabbath School. Keep the elections to a minimum, and then place everyone else into ministries. A minimal goal would be to have at least 60 percent of the attenders involved in ministry of some kind. Keep in mind that one of the prime areas of ministry will be the small group leaders and people involved in felt-need ministries.

Buying Property

A major mistake made by many new churches is to attempt to purchase property during the first year of existence. Do not succumb to that temptation. Wait for at least five years. As soon as a church invests in property, the whole tenor of the church changes. It usually ceases to focus on outreach and instead becomes consumed with buildings and raising money. Funds previously directed to winning the lost are refocused on bricks and mortar. When that happens, most churches cease to grow and lose their effectiveness as agents for extending the kingdom of God.

There may come a time when a congregation will need its own facility, although many churches have discovered that they can continue to grow and expand for many years without owning a facility. In fact, some churches may always rent.

Timing and longevity without buildings is dependent on availability and amenity of local facilities. Also, the longer a church waits to build, the bigger its vision. If it buys property too soon, it is apt to buy too small.

When a church eventually decides that it desires its own facility, how much property should it purchase? It all depends on the vision of the church for its optimal size. The rule of thumb is one acre of land for every one hundred attendees, with a minimum of three acres. This formula is important to follow for the sake of providing sufficient parking for the congregation. Thus, if a church expects someday to have an attendance of five hundred, they should purchase a minimum of five acres. However, if they also project a school to be located at the church, an increased number of acres, consistent with the expected size of the projected school, should also be purchased. However, in an urban area, purchase of land at that rate would be prohibitive. So other options would need to be pursued, especially concerning parking.

If that amount of land is not available or is too expensive, there are alternatives. One of them would be to project two services rather than one. That way a church could get by with less land and still grow to the projected five hundred attendees. Another space saver would be to discover the average number of people who arrive in each car. Today most churches average around two people per vehicle, but experts have projected that in the future the number per car will decrease, thus increasing the need for parking space.

Building problems can consume enormous amounts of time and energy. They are mentioned in this chapter not because they need attention in the first year, but simply as a warning not to be consumed with building during this time. Our plea is to concentrate on building the congregation and not to worry about a building.

The first year of a congregation's life can prove to be one of the most exciting and rewarding times in both the individual and corporate lives of people and church. The excitement of creating something new, the thrill of seeing new people brought to faith in Christ, and the encouragement of watching God's church grow will keep the spiritual fires burning strongly in the hearts of those who have the wonderful opportunity to be a part of the new congregation.

Notes:

1. For a detailed discussion of the Lay Ministry Committee, see the author's book, *Revolution in the Church* (Fallbrook, Calif.: Hart Research Center, 1993), chapter 9.

12

A Plan for Discipleship

The church has started. You have had an excellent response to your first worship service. You have been thrilled to see the same visitors returning week after week. The interests from your evangelistic meeting are becoming regular attenders. Changes in lifestyle are being observed among those newly come to the faith. A baptism has been planned, and several precious people will follow their Lord into the watery grave.

Such a response generates a wellspring of joy within your own heart as you see these people coming to faith in Christ. You anticipate their baptism with joy, but at the same time you are a little apprehensive. What do you do next to ensure that these people become fully devoted followers of Jesus Christ? Most churches rarely plan for anything beyond baptism for their new converts. Yet having a discipleship strategy is absolutely essential if the church is interested in long term maturity among its membership.

A discipleship strategy is a definitive plan into which all new people are asked to enter when they become members of the church. If such a strategy has not been thought through during the prenatal phase of your organization, then it certainly must be done during this first year. In fact, it would be well to have all your nucleus matriculate through the discipleship track. That should guarantee that discipleship will have priority in the new church. It is hard for one who has never been discipled to create disciples. The church planter may have to be the initial discipler, but as the planter moves through the process, others should be trained to disciple.

The mandate of the great commission is to make *disciples*, not simply church members. Therefore the focus of your evangelism strategy should be on the ultimate goal of making disciples and responsible church members rather than on the numerical goal of baptisms, even though baptism is a vital part of the discipleship process. For a full discussion of what is involved in being a disciple, the reader is referred to the author's book *Radical Disciples for Revolutionary Churches.*

Churches need a two-pronged strategy in place for discipleship before the first converts are baptized. First is a general plan of seminars and related activities that will enable the new converts to receive help in their embryonic discipleship endeavors. Second, existing Adventists are personally and individually engaged in helping new converts develop a fruitful life of obedience to Christ.

Four Parts of the General Plan

Rick Warren, in his book *The Purpose Driven Church,*[1] outlines four stages in the discipleship track. He likens this track to a baseball diamond. Each stage of discipleship is relegated to one of the bases. The goal that he suggests is that every new member of the church circle the bases and score, and no one ever be left on base. His analogy is superb and the plan is readily adaptable to an Adventist setting.

To get a person on first base, the church focuses on doing those things that will bring an individual into membership in the Seventh-day Adventist Church. This includes being certain that people have accepted Jesus Christ as their Savior, are trusting fully in Him for salvation, and have the assurance of God's full acceptance. Also, they should have begun to allow Christ to be the Lord of their life and to demonstrate that He is already becoming Lord of their time, money, and bodies. At this stage a person should have a basic acquaintance with the twenty-seven fundamental beliefs of the church and should be baptized and accepted into membership in the body.

Adventists have traditionally done a great job with first base. We know how to get people on board and teach them the basic message of truth. We normally accomplish this through Bible studies, Revelation seminars, Prophecy seminars, and evangelistic crusades. These are a vital necessity, for unless people become members, they probably are not going to be disciples. However, first base is just that—the first step. Traditionally we have had a well-developed first base with very little use of the other bases. We must beware, however, that in our attempt to develop the other bases we do not give less emphasis to first base.

Second base is an attempt to develop the spiritual disciplines, such as prayer, personal Bible study, and a genuine relationship with Jesus. During the developing years of Adventism, most people who joined the Adventist church came from a strong Christian background in another denomination. Therefore, our pioneers did not sense the need to instruct them in the basic elements of Christianity. Yet in the latter part of the twentieth century, and certainly in the twenty-first century, our converts are coming more from a non-Christian background than from another denomination. Therefore we can no longer assume that people understand how to develop spiritual life when they become Adventists. Even those joining from other denominations often have never developed a spiritual life. Remember, George Barna indicated that only 10 percent of the United States population are biblical Christians.[2] It is in the area of spiritual life that most are sorely deficient.

A wise disciple-making church will provide ample opportunities for new people to develop the spiritual disciplines. Seminars that stress a daily walk with Jesus, information on how to study the Bible for beginners, as well as how to have a dynamic prayer life can provide the information that new people desperately need as they begin their walk with Jesus.[3]

Third base attempts to help people discover their spiritual gift(s) and find a place of ministry in the body of Christ in harmony with their giftedness. Part of being a disciple of Jesus is to be involved in ministry. The priesthood of all believers demands that every Christian discover his or her place of ministry in the body of Christ. There is no such thing as an inactive Christian who merely occupies a pew. Christ's radical call unites all believers in actual ministry for the Master.

Development of this base occurs when a church offers its new members spiritual gift seminars that focus on gift discovery and ministry placement.[4] However, more important than actual gift discovery is the placement of the person into a ministry in harmony with that gift. Many churches have conducted excellent spiritual gifts discovery seminars but have failed to follow them up with individual interviews to facilitate people finding a place of ministry in harmony with their giftedness. Since spiritual gifts is one of the twenty-seven fundamental doctrines of the Adventist church, it is surprising that we have been so reticent to develop this base. I have provided much information in this area in my book *Revolution in the Church.*[5] A study of that book may be appropriate for churches that need guidance in developing a lay ministry model based on spiritual gifts.

Home plate focuses on helping new Christians develop a mission focus to their Christian life. Discipleship is never complete until a person has become a disciple maker. In fact, the first two years that a person is in the church is the time that they are most effective in reaching friends and relatives for Christ. After that time most of their close relationships seem to center on church people and thus they become less effective in reaching the lost. It would be important, then, for a church to devise a plan for new people to begin working with their friends and relatives fairly quickly after their own conversion.

This base can be developed through friendship evangelism seminars and by utilizing new people in future evangelistic endeavors.[6] Since they so recently became a part of the church, they have a better understanding of what new people need as they enter the life of the church. It also helps to reconfirm their faith as they hear the message again. Many times new people "spoil" their friends for evangelism by sharing the wrong things too quickly. Therefore it is imperative that the church provide good instruction on evangelism for them as soon as possible after their conversion

In what order should a new person go through the bases? People have to get on first base first, obviously. However, the other bases can be developed in any order, depending upon the needs of the individual who has recently come to faith. Some may be prepared immediately to develop base four and work for their friends, while others may have a more pressing need to develop spiritual life. A wise church will individualize the process as much as possible. The important thing to remember is to get a commitment from new people either before or at the time of their baptism to enter into a plan of discipleship, so that they know this is expected of them. If they get involved in the process, mature faith will begin to develop as they move through the bases.

A Personal Plan

While the general plan that we have just suggested is vitally important for churches to develop, it is not sufficient as a total discipleship plan. In addition, it would be helpful for new people to have a personal mentor who is responsible for their discipleship. This mentor would make certain that the new Christian attended the spiritual development functions offered by the church and would provide regular guidance in the application of the principles learned to the individual life.

For example, the church might provide a seminar on how to study the Bible, but as the new Adventists begin to apply what is learned, questions might develop on whether or not their method of Bible study is correct. The mentor would be available to help provide the guidance needed as people develop their own individual study program. Mentors would not just tell the people what to do but would be trained to ask the right questions to enable the new people to develop their own plan of study. The goal of the mentor should be to help the new Christians fully develop in their spiritual life to the place where they become mentors.

This one-on-one discipleship is difficult because most people have never been mentored in the development of their own spiritual life. They feel awkward about helping others chart a course that they themselves have not taken. There is real risk in it for the mentors, for they may discover that their own life needs spiritual development. The ability to admit that they are not fully developed spiritually and still have room to grow is an essential quality for all mentors.

One of the goals of discipleship is to help individuals reach the place where they are able to live in mutual accountability to other Christians. This does not mean that people are always watching for someone to make a mistake so that they can report it. Accountability means holding one another accountable for our actions without reporting to another person. Mutual accountability is sorely missing in most churches today but is an essential ingredient of being discipled.

One of the best avenues for developing mutual accountability is participation in a relational small group. This was the genius of early Adventism with their "social meetings," where individuals were held accountable for their life in Christ.[7] As Christians meet together regularly in a small group where they share their life in Christ, mutual accountability will develop almost automatically.

One of the goals of a disciple-making church is to encourage all new people to join a small group as soon as possible after baptism if they are not already part of such a group.

Since Christianity is a community-based faith and not an "individualized" religion, involvement in such a relational group should be considered almost mandatory for serious Christians. It is nearly impossible to develop a spiritual life without involvement in some kind of small relational group.

Discipleship

The purpose of this short chapter is not to explore fully a discipleship program for a new church. That might require a whole book.[8] Instead, this chapter has attempted to alert the church planter to the need for developing such a strategy either during the prenatal phase or the first year of existence. Don't allow time to pass without putting a discipleship track into place in the new church. This is one area that it is easy to assume takes place automatically, but it does not. It must be planned.

As a result of having a disciple-making strategy in place in your new church, existing members as well as new members will be advancing to maturity of faith. The visible results of involving your members in this discipleship plan are numerous. People are excited about their faith. They demonstrate love and acceptance of people. Ministry is shared by fellow members of the priesthood of all believers. God is seen as top priority in the lives of His followers. People not only return their tithe, but excitedly give to advance the work of God. New people regularly come to new life in Christ as members share their vibrant faith. Worship is an exciting time, not because of the form, but as a result of the contagious faith of those worshiping.

If this is what you desire for your new church, then by all means develop a disciple-making strategy for it. Then think through how every aspect of the life of your church centers around making disciples. What was described in the preceding paragraph need not be a pipe dream, but a vibrant reality for the church that centers in disciple making.

Notes:

1. Rick Warren, *The Purpose Driven Church: Growth Without Compromising Your Message & Mission* (Grand Rapids: Zondervan, 1995).

2. George Barna, *The Index of Leading Spiritual Indicators* (Dallas: Word, 1996),124-128.

3. An excellent tool for conducting such a seminar is the book *More and Still More* by Joe Engelkemier, available through your Adventist Book Center. This practical book was commissioned for NET '98 to facilitate the development of the spiritual life.

4. One of the best resources for gift discovery and ministry placement is *Connections*, available from Advent Source: (800) 328-0525.

5. Russell Burrill, *Revolution in the Church.*

6. Resources to help develop commitment to mission include Mark Finley's *Making Friends for God: Fulfilling the Gospel Commission* (Fallbrook, Calif.: Hart Research) and Monte Sahlin's seminar on Friendship Evangelism (available through Advent Source [800] 328-0525).

7. For a treatment of the early Adventist social meeting, see the author's book *The Revolutionized Church of the 21st Century.*

8. For those who wish to read further on developing a discipleship strategy, the author recommends Aubrey Malphurs' book *Strategy 2000: Churches Making Disciples for the Next Millennium* (Grand Rapids: Kregel Resources, 1996).

13

Unique Church Plants

Some church plants create churches whose structure is so radically different from traditional churches that planting those kinds of churches requires special attention. Some cutting-edge churches, such as the seeker type churches, do not radically alter the structure of the existing church. In this chapter we wish to explore briefly three unique church plants that *do* affect the structure of the local church in specific ways. Those plants are: non-pastor-dependent churches, lay-led churches, and cell churches.

Non-Pastor-Dependent Churches

This kind of church has a pastor, but the church is designed in such a way that the church is not overly dependent upon the pastor. The pastor is clearly seen as the trainer / equipper / evangelizer, but the pastor does not serve as the shepherd of the flock. We have already suggested that most new churches need to be started in this modality. What follows are a few suggestions to help make certain that this kind of plant takes root.

First, don't begin the plant until the idea of non-pastor-dependency has been thoroughly accepted by the members of the nucleus. Have the pastoral role expectations clearly spelled out in the mission statement to which the whole nucleus has agreed. Begin practicing this model of leadership even during the nucleus-building phase. If the nucleus members are accustomed to ministry being done in the conventional shepherding model, they will expect it to continue in the new church plant. It cannot be emphasized too strongly that the church plant be initiated in the new model of ministry.

Second, spend some time discussing with the nucleus the placement of members into ministry and whether or not this is going to be a requirement for membership in the body. Will there be a different standard of membership for those joining from other Seventh-day Adventist churches than for new converts? To what membership standards will you adhere in addition to agreement with the twenty-seven fundamental beliefs? How strictly will your group adhere to these additional ministry requirements?

How will ministry placement occur? How will you identify people's spiritual gifts? After identification, how will you go about placing people into ministry in harmony with their giftedness? It is important during the nucleus-building phase to thoroughly discuss and have in place a plan for new people to get involved before the first service of the new church is held. Other areas to discuss include the length of time that people are placed in a specific ministry. How can they get out if they feel have been misplaced? How can they be removed if you feel they have been misplaced? Have a clear set of guidelines before you start the church. In the conventional church, this is cared for by the yearly nominating committee. In the non-pastor-dependent church, where people are placed into more permanent ministries, solutions to problems need to be thought through before a crisis arises. So have a clear plan of action written out and in place that everyone understands from the beginning.

Third, in the nucleus-building phase you need to discuss

the place of the nominating committee. While nominating committees may not play as large a role in this kind of church, some form of this committee needs to be in place. Our suggestion has been to limit the nominating committee to those whom you are holding accountable for the church, presumably the church board. It would be a sad mistake to eliminate the nominating committee completely. The consequence of this would be that power would be confined to a very small group of people who could control the entire church and possibly even direct the church in the wrong way. You may decide to streamline your church board, but make certain that there are key lay people who are elected by the whole congregation each year. The lay ministry committee can place people into ministry in harmony with their giftedness, but the nominating committee must elect people to serve as officers of the church.

In this area, it would be well to keep the conference clearly informed of your different structure. To move into a lay ministry structure may mean doing church differently from what the church manual suggests. Therefore, it is imperative that you keep the conference notified of your change in structure. Most conferences are willing to work with pastors who are trying new paradigms, but they appreciate being kept informed.

The fourth area of concern when planting this kind of church is the care of the membership. In the non-pastor-dependent church, the pastor is not the chief caregiver. Therefore, care of existing members needs to be arranged by some other medium. The pastor may participate in that care but cannot be the chief caregiver. Some churches design their church around small groups who care for the members. This works fine for many people, but in most churches there are many people who do not join groups and thus can slip between the cracks. During the nucleus-building phase, make certain that you discuss this whole issue of pastoral care and have in writing a plan for all members to be cared for in the new church.

Lay-Led Churches

Much of what has been said about non-pastor-dependent churches also applies to the lay-led church. However, there are some unique characteristics of this church, as well, that need attention. With no salaried person in place, it is even more necessary that this church plant depend upon good lay volunteers.

The first consideration is to visit with the conference officials and make certain that they agree with you in the formation of this kind of church. Don't be surprised if they ask many specific questions. They need to ask them, for you are forming a church that does not have a conference employee in charge. That church will bear the name "Seventh-day Adventist," and the conference is responsible to make certain that the church will adequately represent the Adventist faith.

The conference will want to understand specifically why you wish to start this kind of church, what your plans are for handling the tithe and other conference funds, your theology and understanding of Adventists beliefs, and who from the conference is going to be in charge. They may even want to reserve the right to appoint the person that they will hold responsible for the church. Expect some very definitive questions in each of these areas.

Let us now suppose that the conference has given its approval for the formation of your lay-led church. During the nucleus-building phase, you will need to work through the organizational structure upon which your church will operate. Without a pastor or paid employee in charge, you will need to decide how the work will be divided. Do not assume that whoever the conference appoints is the sole leader and become "leader dependent" upon this person. In order for a lay-led church to thrive, leadership must be shared among several individuals in the congregation. In fact, the church will need to operate under the direction of a council of elders rather than a single individual.

Other factors to deal with include how the membership is going to be cared for without a paid leader, how evangelism is going to be done, etc. Follow the counsel given for non-pastor-dependent churches in the previous section. If you are the appointed leader, you will need to arrange to report to someone in the conference office. (However, even though you may be the appointed leader from the conference, leadership really is shared.) It is very important to keep communication channels open to conference leadership so they continually know what is happening. Such openness will enable you to receive a lot of excellent counsel as you seek to plant a lay-led Adventist church on a solid foundation.

Cell Churches

The most radical organizational shift in church planting occurs when one decides to plant a cell church. This kind of church is very different from the existing structure that most Adventists are used to; therefore, special training is required in order to understand the dynamics of creating this unique style of church.

First, one must do extensive reading and receive adequate training before the cell church plant is begun.[1] This method of conducting church is so different that the usual procedure for organizing a church does not apply. For example, a cell church has no traditional officers such as elder, deacon, personal ministries leader, etc. The structure is and must be totally different when planting such a church.

Second, understand the difference between a cell church and a church with small groups. Many who have attempted to plant a cell church have really planted a church with small groups. These are two entirely different kinds of churches. In a cell church, the church is totally organized around the small groups. People cannot even join the church unless they belong to a group. In small group churches, membership in the group is viewed as desirable but optional. In cell churches, the church is complete in the cell and does not need all the groups meeting together to be the church. A cell is not part of the church; it *is* the church.

There are two ways in which cell churches are organized. One is built on the "Jethro model" of the Old Testament. In this model each small group has a leader and an apprentice leader. There is a lay leader over every five groups, a zone pastor over every twenty-five groups, and a senior pastor over the entire church. The size of the church determines whether the zone pastor is needed in addition to the senior pastor. This model favors heavy pastoral supervision, but has worked fairly well with developing cell churches.

The second model of cell church is in the developing stage, but promises an approach that is less pastor dependent. It has been called the G-12 structure and is built somewhat on the Jesus discipleship model. Just as Jesus chose twelve people to disciple who in turn will disciple others, so the G-12 structures groups of people by twelve. The initial cell of twelve people are thoroughly discipled, and then each one moves out as a cell leader and forms a group of twelve whom they will disciple. Thus the one cell multiples into twelve cells immediately. Each leader of the cell stays in the original cell, but at the same time becomes the leader of another group of twelve. Once the new group is fully discipled, they, too, move out and form their group of twelve. This model holds tremendous potential for a massive evangelistic explosion. It does require each person to be in two cells each week, one in which they are a member and the other that they lead. It assumes that every person is a potential leader and needs to be discipled to disciple others.

The cell church, especially in the G-12 structure, is built around discipleship. In fact, the discipleship track is the distinguishing sign of the cell church. Churches with small groups usually do not have such a heavy discipleship track. Utilizing the cell church approach, especially the G-12 structure, results in explosive evangelism, and also every member becomes fully discipled and is placed in leadership as the leader of a small group.

Because of the cell organization in this kind of church, the usual church offices do not exist. The church does not run traditional programs, not even traditional Sabbath Schools. Most of its activities and mission work originate out of the cells rather than the whole body. This can be very confusing to a conference office that desires to communicate with the various program leaders. In the cell church there are no program leaders. To run a cell church in a conference will necessitate lengthy and frequent communication with conference officials as the details are worked out.

This brief overview of cell organization should be enough to convince anyone who desires to start a cell church to seek the needed help to make certain the new church is formed correctly. In fact, no conference should allow anyone who has not been through certified cell church training to start a cell church. Yet, at the same time, cell churches could be the source of tremendous new growth in Adventism if allowed to create some new wineskins for the timeless truths of God's word.

Notes:

1. Suggested books to begin reading on the cell church are Ralph W. Neighbour, Jr., *Where Do We Go From Here?* (Houston, TX: Touch, 1990), and William A. Beckham, *The Second Reformation* (Houston, TX: Touch, 1997). Training seminars are regularly conducted by NADEI. Information may be obtained by calling NADEI at (616) 471-9220 or visiting the web page at *www.nadei.org*.

14

Financing the New Congregation

All of this church planting sounds fascinating, but how are we going to pay for all these new churches? This is a question heard by many who have advocated the planting of new churches. The picture that many conjure up is one costing thousands of dollars. The reason for that high cost is the belief that church planting requires a new pastor who will serve a church that will not produce enough tithe for pastoral support, and that the newly planted church will need to construct a new building to house their congregation.

We have attempted to shatter these arguments throughout this book by suggesting that a new church plant need not require a hired pastor. Planting non-pastor-dependent churches and lay-led churches would eliminate the need to hire so many clergy. Yet, many church plants will require a clergy person. We have also cautioned against building too soon. Although rental cost is a factor, construction should not occur for several years into the plant, and therefore building cost should not be considered as a cost of church planting.

When we think of financial resources, we have a tendency to think only of existing resources, and they always come up short. Instead, realize that the money needed for pastoral coverage and a new building are to be found in the harvest that will be gathered. It is a mistake to think that new congregations need to be continually subsidized. That creates a dependency situation that is not healthy for the church. The new church should qualify for a building subsidy just as any other congregation in the conference, but it needs no special funding for building. The people that have been won to Christ in the new church can provide the needed funding for the building.

Church planting does not require raising a lot of additional revenue; it can generate much of its own resources out of the harvest that is reached. An initial investment may be necessary to get the new congregation off the ground, but usually the investment will be returned with interest in a very short period of time. Denominations that spend huge amounts of money on church plants do not plant very many churches; whereas denominations that spend minimum dollars on the church plant are planting hundreds of new churches. Adventists need to learn how to plant churches inexpensively. Those who plant expensively usually spend significant dollars in providing a building and paying for the salary. But neither of these areas need to consume the finances of the denomination.

Funding Pastoral Salaries

This is perhaps the biggest financial issue in starting new congregations. There are several solutions to the money problem regarding pastoral salaries for new church plants. First, planting lay-led churches eliminates the need to provide pastoral coverage and has the added benefit of providing tithe dollars to a conference with little or no expense. Wise conferences will not utilize that extra money into the regular denominational expense pocket but will funnel those monies back into church planting, either into other lay-led plants or to provide pastoral salaries for new church plants.

Ideally, when pastors are hired to church plant, they should be sent forth in teams of two or more. Any major church plant would best be started with a team rather than solo workers. However, teams are expensive. For many conferences, it is difficult to find the money for *one* pastor to church plant in an area. To find money for two seems impossible. Yet Jesus commanded us to go forth two by two. We cannot afford to disregard His counsel. If a conference attempts to find the money as an add-on to existing projects, it probably will never happen.

Instead, the conference will need to find a way to free up money for the church planting project. It is a matter of priorities. If church planting is the priority of the conference, then church planting will receive priority in funding. Back in chapter 3 we examined early Adventist church planting and proposed a modern solution in harmony with our heritage.

That solution entailed the creation of fifteen to twenty churches in a district, headed by a "mini" conference president who would train, equip, and coach the lay leaders in each of the churches. The monies saved by this combining of churches would be reinvested in church planting, especially in the great urban centers. This approach would allow the conference to utilize a team approach to church planting, in harmony with the counsel of Jesus.

Other solutions could be followed to provide pastoral help in church planting. One is the bi-vocational pastor. Here individuals are hired on a stipend basis to start a church, but it is expected that they will work at another occupation part time. In the past, some have taught school or colporteured while engaged in church planting, but bi-vocational pastors need not be limited to those fields. In some situations the church may never grow large enough to warrant its own full-time pastor, in which case the bi-vocational church planter would forever continue in that venue. Or the church could be incorporated into a multi-church district.

Another variation of the bi-vocational model is the hiring

of a planter on a stipend, with the understanding that the stipend will continue to increase as new tithe monies are generated. The stipend would be based on 30 percent of the annual tithe (or whatever percentage of tithe the local conference uses for pastoral salaries). For example, the conference agrees to support the church planter for the first two years at $1,000 per month with no other benefits. After the second year, the planter would receive 30 percent of new tithe generated. We suggest new tithe, so that the planter is not tempted to simply recruit many people from existing churches and create a false sense of growth. The new tithe is from the harvest—new converts or non-tithe-paying Adventists who have been reclaimed. In this model the conference loses nothing, but gains from the church plant.

We suggest two years of conference support, since the first year is going to be spent creating the nucleus and laying the foundation for the new plant. Therefore, in the first year there would be only a few months in which the new church would be operating and not enough time to indicate an annual tithe basis. However, at the end of the second year sufficient time would have elapsed to create a tithe basis for remuneration as suggested above.

Let's suppose that during the second year the new church had produced $50,000 in new tithe. That is not unrealistic for a harvest-centered church. The local conference allocates 30 percent of tithe for pastoral salaries. For the third year the stipend of the worker would be based on $15,000, an increase of $3,000 a year. Each year the stipend would increase until the planter reached full salary. This method would allow a conference to sponsor many church plants with very little investment.

Some of these plants will not take. If after two years insufficient tithe revenue has been produced to increase the stipend and the church is not growing, other alternatives will need to be followed. The plant could be closed and the new members asked to move to other area churches. If there are not other nearby churches, the new group could be made a part of a large district, where it would basically care for itself. This should be clearly indicated at the beginning, before the church plant is started, so that there will be no misunderstanding at the end of the first two years.

In this section we have explored ways to fund pastoral salaries in church plants. We have singled out this area of financing because it is the biggest obstacle to church planting in most people's minds. It certainly is the biggest expense involved. However, as we have suggested, there can be innovative and creative ways to provide for pastoral coverage, where desired, without utilizing new funding.

Perhaps we need to be frank at this point. We have talked about the priority of the harvest in this book, the great need for church planting in the major urban centers. No one will deny that this should be a priority of the Church. Our Adventist heritage declares that we were born and nourished as a church planting movement. Yet we spend most of our time trying to find a way to do it without it costing us anything. Perhaps we need to begin at that level, but we must move deeper.

If church planting to reach the lost is the priority of Adventism, then we must take a careful look at how we are spending God's tithe in relationship to the needs of the harvest. And not only the tithe, but our offerings as well. If we truly believe this to be the end time, then we need to start acting as if it were the end time by reordering the priorities of the Church to reflect the priority of God for the harvest. Perhaps we can no longer afford to spend 95 percent of our monies on ourselves and only 5 percent for the harvest of God. It may mean that there are certain services which the Church is currently providing that can no longer be provided in view of God's passion for reaching the lost. Or it may be that we will need to discover a way to do those things in such a way that they will not consume so much of the resources of the Church.

It's time to put our money where our mouth is. We need to stop verbalizing our belief in church planting as a priority and begin to demonstrate that it *is* the priority by placing needed funding into starting hundreds of new churches. This is not a plea for expensive church planting. As has been already suggested, that would be harmful to church planting. The more we subsidize a new plant, the more dependent it becomes, and ultimately the less productive it is. Yet the basic funding must be there to get it going.

One of the smaller union conferences in North America decided to make church planting a real priority. They sold their union office and built a smaller one. Out of the proceeds from the sale, they put aside $800,000 for church planting. Not all offices can or should be sold, but all unions and conferences can find the needed money if they make it a priority.

Other Funding

Pastoral coverage and evangelism budgets have been the responsibility of the local conferences in Adventism. That should continue. However, other monies are going to be needed in order to successfully plant a new church. This would include the funds needed for the regular operation of the new church, such as rental facilities, felt-need outreach, supplies, etc. Where does the money come from for these expenses? From the people involved in the church plant.

The conference should have little if any participation in any expense for church planting beyond the traditional cost for pastoral coverage and evangelism budgets. Otherwise they will over-subsidize the new congregation and create a weak church. This means that stewardship must be taught to the new members from the very beginning. Many church planters have been negligent here. They have failed to teach biblical stewardship, and the result has been that the churches become overly dependent upon subsidies and thus become weak. This is the result of planters being disobedient to their biblical mandate to follow the example of Jesus and teach people about the priority of money for the kingdom of God.

When biblical stewardship is taught and practiced in new churches, there will be no lack of money for needed expenses at the local level. As new members are taught tithing, they will begin returning a faithful tithe, which will provide the needed funding for pastoral salaries. Even before the new plant gets started, stewardship should be taught and practiced among the members of the nucleus, so that funding is provided for many of the start-up costs encountered in beginning the new church.

Money is rarely a problem in the Adventist church. If we are really committed to a project, we find the money needed. It is a matter of priorities. This is not to deny that there are monetary challenges associated with church planting—there are. But through personal sacrifice and commitment, these challenges can be met successfully.

Organizing the New Church

Seventh-day Adventist churches are not incorporated institutions. The legal affairs of the local church are cared for through the local conference association. Therefore the church planter does not incorporate the newly planted church, but works through the local conference. Briefly, here is the procedure to follow.

1. Before beginning the new congregation, the planter works in harmony with the local conference so that the conference has already approved of the formation of the new group. No other action is necessary until the church has its first public service.

2. When the church is ready to go public, the conference should be contacted to discover what organizational procedure the church should pursue as it enters its public phase. There are two possibilities: to be organized as an official company or as a full-fledged church.

Most conferences prefer to organize a new group as a company. Then, after membership and tithe have reached a certain level and the church has proven to be a viable entity, they organize it as a church. However, if the initial group appears to be very vibrant, some conferences will bypass the company stage of organization and move immediately into the church organization. That's why the planter should contact the conference to discover the procedure to follow when they are ready for their first organizational step.

The difference between a church and a company is that a church can elect its own officers, whereas in a company the officers are appointed by the conference. In a church, the membership is held in the local church, but in the company stage the membership is held in the conference church and the conference committee is responsible for all membership issues, such as transferring or discipline. After a church has existed as a company for awhile and the church has stabilized with sufficient membership and tithe base, the planter should contact the conference for counsel on when to organize as an official church.

Both company and church organization usually are facilitated with a public ceremony with conference officials present. The planter should counsel with the conference as plans are made for this organizational service. Once the organizational service is over, the church is considered organized. However a formal action is required at the next conference constituency meeting to officially vote the church into the sisterhood of churches. For more detailed information on company or church organization, read the church manual and the minister's manual.

It is important for the local church to proceed with these organizational plans, as the church has no legal status for giving tax-deductible receipts or other legal issues except through its organization in the local conference. Working with the local conference officials is vital for the planter at this point, and most conference officials are very anxious to help facilitate the organization of new churches.

15

Creating Healthy Churches

If you have read this far, you probably are excited about church planting and wish to be involved in a church plant, either as a participant or as a sponsoring church. However, this book is not about just planting churches—it is also about planting *healthy* churches. Some are so desirous of planting churches that they fail to plant legitimate, healthy Adventist churches. That is not the intention of this book.

As we began this adventure we attempted to make clear that our focus is on reaching the harvest with Adventism's special message. If that is to happen, we must plant healthy churches that are true to the teachings of Adventism. We must not compromise our message in order to reach people with the gospel, even though we must indigenize that message to each target group. They must accept untarnished, uncompromised Adventism

We feel that God has called this church into being to give the unique message of the three angels as the final warning message to planet Earth. Every Adventist church must therefore make prominent those unique and special messages that have nurtured this church during the last one-and-a-half centuries. That message centers on the three angels' messages of Revelation 14:6-12. It is inconceivable that anyone would form an Adventist church that does not agree with those messages and that would not clearly present them in a Christ-centered evangelistic approach.

Adventism has room for much diversity. Yet there are certain areas that are non-negotiable. These landmarks of Adventism have been clearly defined by Ellen White:

> The passing of the time in 1844 was a period of great events, opening to our astonished eyes the cleansing of the sanctuary transpiring in heaven, and having decided relation to God's people upon the earth, [also] the first and second angels' messages and the third, unfurling the banner on which was inscribed, "The commandments of God and the faith of Jesus." One of the landmarks under this message was the temple of God, seen by His truth-loving people in heaven, and the ark containing the law of God. The light of the Sabbath of the fourth commandment flashed its strong rays in the pathway of the transgressors of God's law. The non-immortality of the wicked is an old landmark. I can call to mind nothing more that can come under the head of the old landmarks. All this cry about changing the old landmarks is all imaginary.[1]

There are five landmarks of Adventism delineated in this passage:

1. The sanctuary message
2. The three angels' messages
3. The law of God
4. The seventh-day Sabbath
5. The nonimmortality of the wicked

These five landmarks are immovable. Any church that does not subscribe to these basic, unique points of Adventism can not rightfully claim to be an Adventist church. Ellen White was also clear that nothing could be added to this list. These are the essential landmarks for an Adventist church.

Adventism today also has the twenty-seven fundamental beliefs of the church. Many of these are an expansion of the five landmarks, plus a declaration of basic Christianity. Ellen White was not defining the essence of the Christian faith but the essence of the Adventist expression of Christianity. Our allegiance to the pillars of Christianity is clearly spelled out in the twenty-seven fundamental beliefs. Thus, a church claiming to be Adventist must subscribe to the non-negotiable pillars and the twenty-seven fundamental beliefs that encompass both our understanding of Adventism and Christianity. It is incomprehensible that a church would desire to be Adventist if it did not agree with this elementary level, yet evidently some wish an abbreviated Adventism. Church planting is not about abbreviated Adventism, but Adventism that is uncompromisingly committed to the true and complete message entrusted to it by God. Any church that does not agree on these points should be denied the privilege of organizing as an Adventist church.

In addition to agreement on these basic doctrines, all Adventist churches should be supportive of the church structure and be loyal financially to that structure. Adventism views itself as a worldwide movement in harmony with Revelation 14:6. It cannot support a congregational approach to ministry and still remain the vital world movement that God has commissioned it to be. This does not mean that the structure cannot be improved upon, but that improvement must be sought within the structure. Any church organized as an Adventist congregation must display loyalty on this point.

Beyond these basic areas of agreement, there will be and must be much diversity in Adventism. Most arguments among Adventists usually focus on areas not covered by the pillars, the twenty-seven beliefs, or the structure. These arguments occur because people desire to move a fringe area into the core area of belief. Adventism must hold firm on these three areas, but at the same time be open for new expressions of the faith to develop in the nonessential areas. Any church formed that is not in harmony with these three areas is not a healthy Adventist church.

Defining Healthy Churches

While the above three areas are essential in order for a church to be healthy, there is much more to it than that. In this chapter we will explore what a healthy church will look like. As we do so, we will be assuming the above three components are present; therefore, we will not refer to them again.

One of the most important pieces of research produced for the Christian church at the end of the twentieth century is the work of Christian Schwarz.[2] In his research, Schwarz examined over a thousand churches on every continent on planet Earth. Through this study he discovered that healthy churches are growing churches and that churches grow best when they do not work on growing. Instead, they concentrate on being healthy, because it is natural for healthy things to grow. He defines natural church development in this way: "Releasing the growth automatisms, by which God Himself grows His church."[3]

When one thinks about it, all nature grows in this way. The flowers, the birds, and even humans do not grow by working on growing—they grow "all by themselves." No wonder Jesus declared:

> The kingdom of God is as if a man should scatter seed on the ground, and should sleep by night and rise by day, and the seed should sprout and grow, he himself does not know how. For the earth yields crops by itself; first the blade, then the head, after that the full grain in the head. But when the grain ripens, immediately he puts in the sickle, because the harvest has come.[4]

> Consider the lilies of the field, how they grow: they neither toil nor spin; and yet I say to you that even Solomon in all his glory was not arrayed like one of these.[5]

Schwarz presents a convincing argument that the best way to grow a church is to grow it in Jesus' style: "all by itself."

Do not concentrate on growing but instead work on those proven areas of church life that create healthy churches. As churches concentrate on building these quality features into the churches that are planted, growth will occur automatically. Schwarz identified eight quality characteristics that are found in healthy churches. Each of these has strong biblical roots. He discovered that when a church reached a certain level in each of the eight quality characteristics, without exception they were growing churches.[6]

Eight Quality Characteristics

Each of Schwarz's eight quality characteristics consists of a noun with a descriptive adjective. The key is not the noun, but the adjective. These eight quality characteristics are listed below with a brief description:[7]

1. Empowering Leadership. Pastors of growing churches are not dictators but people who truly attempt to help others reach their potential for Christ. The leadership style of this kind of pastor empowers people in their ministries.

2. Gift-Oriented Ministry. Growing, healthy churches help their members discover their gifts and find ministry placement in harmony with that giftedness. The structure of the church is thus built around spiritual gifts rather than officers who rule.

3. Passionate Spirituality. Spirituality is alive and well among the members of healthy churches. However, it is not just that members pray and study the Word but they are passionate about that experience. The spiritual life of these kinds of church is strong.

4. Functional Structures. The structures (committees, organizations, plans, etc.) of the local church actually support its mission. In other words, healthy churches don't maintain a program simply because they have always done it. They continually evaluate to make sure they are accomplishing what the church was designed to accomplish.

5. **Inspiring Worship Service**. Because there is passionate spirituality in the church, the members' worship experience rings with authenticity. There is no one kind of service that is needed for this characteristic. Both contemporary and traditional services meet the test. The key ingredient is that it is an inspiring experience, no matter what the style.

6. **Holistic Small Groups**. Healthy churches provide a setting where members can share their life in Christ. These holistic small groups provide the basis for meaningful relationships to develop within the body of Christ. Healthy churches see small groups as a necessity rather than an option.

7. **Need-Oriented Evangelism**. Healthy churches recognize that while all Christians are witnesses, God has uniquely gifted certain individuals with the gift of evangelism. Growing, healthy churches have identified these people as well as helping all Christians focus on witnessing to the people in their networks.

8. **Loving Relationships**. Growing, healthy churches are majoring in helping people develop loving relationships within the body. In these kinds of churches a basic trust level is developed where people no longer highly criticize each other. The result is the release of happiness and joy in the congregation.

Schwarz suggests that a church should discover how well it is doing in each of the eight quality characteristics.[8] After assessing each area, he recommends that a church begin working on its "minimum factor," identified as the characteristic with the lowest score. He suggests that in order for the church to begin to grow, it must work on the minimum factor.

Those who wish to understand these concepts more fully should read Schwarz' research in *Natural Church Development* and *The Implementation Guide to Natural Church Development*.

Planting Healthy Churches

Since research has shown that these eight quality characteristics must exist in a church if it is to be healthy and growing, church planters would be wise to make certain that each of the eight elements are built into the new church being developed. Not only are these eight qualities based upon research, but they also have a very strong biblical base. For example, gift-based ministry is clearly built around Ephesians 4:7-16. In other words, modern research has substantiated what the New Testament advocates as the ideal of ministry for Christians. Another example would be loving relationships. Jesus declared that everyone would know that Christians are His disciples if they loved one another.[9] This strong biblical root can be substantiated for most of the eight quality characteristics.

As a church is being planted, it would be helpful to work through the *Implementation Guide to Natural Church Development* to make certain each of the principles are being embodied into the life of the new church. In this way the nucleus group will quickly learn what is the minimum factor in their group so that they can begin to work on that area before the church is planted. Ideally, all eight quality characteristics should be in place when a church is planted.

Rather than working on growing, this process envisions the church concentrating on creating the quality that both Scripture and research indicate needs to be present in the church. Once the quality is there, growth will occur automatically. Creating quality churches releases the power of God to grow the church instead of focusing on human effort.

This chapter has attempted to provide a brief overview of the concepts described in *Natural Church Development*. Our focus here is not to present the concept in its entirety, since that is adequately done in Schwarz' works. Instead, our purpose is to acquaint the church planter with this very significant research and suggest that wise planters will avail themselves of this material, study it, and begin to implement it in the new church that they are planting. Wise church planters will plant healthy Adventist churches that not only are faithful in doctrine but are healthy in the qualities examined here.

Notes:

1. Ellen G. White, *Counsels to Writers and Editors* (Hagerstown: Review and Herald, 1946), 30, 31.

2. Christian Schwarz, *Natural Church Development* (Chicago: Church Smart, 1996).

3. Ibid., 3.

4. Mark 4:26-29 (NKJV).

5. Matt. 6:28, 29 (NKJV).

6. Schwarz, 40.

7. For a fuller understanding of these eight quality characteristics, see Schwarz, pages 22-37.

8. An instrument to enable a church to discover how well it is doing in each of the eight quality characteristics can be utilized. The results of the questionnaire can be entered into the computer and compared with the other churches in Schwarz' study. There is a charge for this service. For information, contact NADEI, 9047 US 31 North, Suite 3, Berrien Springs, MI 49103. Telephone: (616) 471-9220, or e-mail: 104100.20@compuserve.com.

9. John 13:15.

16

Recreating a Church Planting Movement

Seventh-day Adventism was born and grew as a church planting movement. While the Church in North America can no longer claim church planting as a distinction, Adventist church planting is flourishing in much of the world. Yet the need for church planting still exists in North America. In fact, North America is one of the greatest mission fields on planet Earth today. In order to reach the final harvest that God intended when He raised up the Adventist church, many more churches will need to be planted. North American Adventism will need to become a church planting movement once again.

What will it take to return North American Adventism to a church planting multiplication movement? In this chapter we wish to explore the necessary ingredients.[1] We will also explore ways in which these ingredients can become a vital part of North American Adventism.

What Is a Reproducible System?

Reproducible systems are self-generating. As Schwarz indicated in his research, churches need to learn to grow naturally. He also indicates that churches need to begin thinking in a different way, using what he calls "biotic principles." He suggests six such principles, one of which is "multiplication."[2]

> The principle of multiplication applies to all areas of church life: Just as the true fruit of an apple tree is not an apple, but another tree; the true fruit of a small group is not a new Christian, but another group; the true fruit of a church is not a new group, but a new church; the true fruit of a leader is not a follower, but a new leader; the true fruit of an evangelist is not a convert, but new evangelists. Whenever this principle is understood and applied, the results are dramatic.[3]

A reproducible system is one in which reproduction is built into every level. As a result, the harvest is continually increasing through the multiplication of all levels: individual disciples, cell leaders, pastors, church planters, evangelists, and leaders. A reproducible system is always concerned with duplication. A church planting reproducible system is not concerned with church planting only but with reproduction throughout the entire system. For example, if we concentrated only on reproducing churches and not on reproducing the entire system, there would be no leaders for the new churches. On the other hand, however, if leaders are constantly being reproduced throughout the system, new leadership will be continually available for new church plants. That is what is meant by recreating a reproducing church planting movement—one that continually feeds upon itself.

In a true reproducible system, no one is placed into leadership who has not demonstrated the ability to reproduce. It is the one quality that must be demonstrated before a person is assigned a leadership position. In other words, do not make anyone the leader of a small group who has not previously won at least one convert to Christ. Likewise, do not place an individual in leadership over several small groups who has never multiplied a small group. In the same manner, never call a person to be a pastor who has never been in leadership over multiplying groups. The whole system must support reproduction.

This scenario would place a great number of current leaders out of a job. However, no system changes overnight. Current leaders will need to be trained into the new paradigm that values reproduction. However, the process can begin with the hiring of new leaders. Interviews conducted as part of the hiring process will need to search for leadership qualities in the area of reproduction. Even new Christians can be examined in this area, for they do not necessarily have to be experienced in soul winning. In their secular life there would be a demonstration of the leadership qualities needed in the area of reproduction.

To create a reproducible system, every aspect of church life must be scrutinized in order to discover how to ensure reproduction from it. As someone has observed: "We don't just need the golden egg; we need the goose that lays the golden egg." That goose is a reproducible system. Yet many pastors have had a tendency to think of themselves either as called to plant new churches or called to strengthen existing churches. This is not an either/or situation. In a reproducible system, both need to be accomplished. In other words, churches are strengthened in order that they may reproduce, for only healthy growing churches can fulfill the ultimate command of God to "be fruitful and multiply."[4]

Dr. Robert E. Logan suggests that there are six components to a reproducible system:

1. A plan to mobilize regional strategic intercession for church planting.

2. A plan to raise up workers and leaders for the harvest from the harvest.

3. A plan to multiply cell groups.

4. A plan to resource church planters and new churches so that they continue to grow.

5. A plan to facilitate churches planting churches, so that churches themselves become reproducing systems.

6. A plan to refocus existing congregations so they continue the reproduction cycle.[5]

How to Accomplish a Reproducible System in Adventism

Most of us can look at these six points and heartily agree that it would be nice for them to exist in the Seventh-day Adventist Church. Yet in reality most of us feel that to accomplish this in Adventism would be extremely difficult. That is the stark reality in which we find ourselves. Adventism in North America at the beginning of the millennium bears only slight resemblance to the grand design of the reproducible system as advocated by Logan. Yet down deep each of us wishes that somehow it could be accomplished.

The good news is that it is not impossible for the Seventh-day Adventist Church to become a reproducible system! It may necessitate a lot of work and tough times, but if we persevere, it can happen. God is with the Adventist church, and His great desire is to see it succeed in the mission to which He has called it. Thus, while from a human perspective it seems impossible, yet from the divine perspective it becomes reachable. Logan has counseled us where to begin.

At the conclusion of Seeds '97, Logan remarked that when a denomination discovers it is no longer as effective in reaching the harvest as it once was, the answer to regaining its effectiveness lies in its history. If the denomination will carefully examine what it did in its early days that made it such a mighty instrument of God, it will usually discover what it needs to do in order to once again become a mighty avenue for the outpouring of God's Spirit. The answer lies in our history.

In the early part of this book we examined early Adventist history. There we discovered a vibrant movement, led by God, that valued the harvest. The priority of the church was reaching the harvest, and all of its resources were allocated for that purpose. Thus, we discovered that pastors were primarily church planters and evangelists rather than caregivers. Perhaps this rediscovery of the pastoral role will enable the present-day church to recapture the priorities of the early days.

No, we cannot replicate the nineteenth century in the twenty-first century, but we can learn from it and apply the principles to the church today. After hearing the author speak about creating fifteen church districts with small churches in order to free up pastors for church planting, especially in the urban areas, some have remarked that the churches simply will not buy into the idea. Some have even called it foolish thinking. They may be right if we are thinking only of the present church. Most churches today are very self-centered and want their share of the pie. In that kind of environment, creating fifteen church districts *is* impossible.

However, if the churches understand early Adventist history and the counsel of Ellen White regarding pastors hovering over the churches, and if they clearly understand that they serve under the emblem of the One who commissioned them to reach the harvest, they will do whatever is necessary to be obedient to the Master they love. In other words, we must recreate a mission mentality in the churches so that a change to the fifteen-church district, for example, is not legislated but *demanded* by the churches themselves, for they see it as an act of obedience to their risen Lord.

The author has observed that when the churches are educated and when this mission mentality has been established, those small churches are willing to be part of a new paradigm, including a fifteen-church district, in order to reach the harvest. This difference in attitude has been created because the church now possesses a new priority: the gathering in of the harvest. Therefore, the first step in moving North American Adventism to a reproducible system is the creation of a mission mindset in the churches of North America. Obviously, this will not occur overnight and will not happen universally en masse. Any movement begins small and spreads. So with the movement to create a reproducible system.

As this new century opens, the North American Adventist Church stands at the threshold of a fresh beginning: the education of pastors, churches, and conferences in church planting and a reproducible system. In fact, the idea of church planting has caught on very well and many new churches are being planted. But that is only the beginning. Many who have "bought in" to church planting have not yet seen the necessity for creating the reproducible system. That is what the educational phase is all about.

What methods can be used to educate into the paradigm of reproduction? The Seeds Conferences have been helping to create this vision. In addition, pastors' meetings and lay people's congresses are being conducted, educating people into these new concepts. The seminary and the educational system, the conference administrators and departments, all need education into the new paradigm. Part of the educational process involves articles in denominational magazines, books like this one, newsletters, and a host of other mechanisms for creating a mission mentality and the reproducible system in the Adventist church in North America.

While the education process goes a long way toward helping the church become a multiplication system, much more than education is necessary. Certain structural changes will be required to facilitate the accomplishment of the new mission mentality. This is where it gets difficult, but only because we attempt to move to phase two before we have accomplished phase one. Once the mission mentality is in place, structural change will occur much more easily. That does not mean it will not be traumatic, but it will be much easier to accomplish in the midst of a mission mentality.

A Church Planting Multiplication System

Logan suggests several structural elements that need to be built into a church planting reproduction system.[6] The first is what he calls "New Church Incubators." This organization occurs up through the first year of a church's existence. Its function is to guide church planters, their spouses, and key leaders through the process of starting a healthy new church. A coach is needed to work with these church planters on a regular basis. The coach would also help the church to discover the resources it needs to accomplish the start. In the "New Church Incubator" the leaders come together monthly to learn from each other and from the coach. In between monthly meetings the coach visits personally with each planter, giving support at least every two weeks. The loneliest worker in the denomination is the church planter. The only person lonelier than the planter is the planter's spouse.

The only personnel needed for the New Church Incubator is the coach. In the early stages, this person could be hired on the union level. The coach would then work with a New Church Incubator in each conference in the union (assuming a maximum of five conferences). All the beginning church planters in one conference would then be together in a New Church Incubator. As church planting increases in a union, it might be necessary to hire more than one coach or move the coaching position to the conference level. As of this writing, two unions have jointly hired one individual for this kind of responsibility. The biggest question is the funding of the coach. However, as planting churches and creating a reproducible system become priorities in the church and in the conference, funding will cease to be a major obstacle. We will do what we prioritize to do.

A second structure that will be needed as church planting grows in a conference is what Logan calls the "New Church Network." This is a grouping of churches that are in years one through three of existence. It groups these new churches together to provide help for their questions and needs. The problems of the one- to three-year-old church are different from the problems of the start-up church. The issue of multiplication must be built into the church during this period or it will not become part of a multiplication system. Coaches must be well educated in helping these churches place multiplication into their "DNA." Every church in a multiplication system should be planting their first church by three to five years of age. The New Church Networks enable this to become reality.

How often should the New Church Networks meet? This would vary, depending on the needs, but the minimum should be once a quarter for a leadership meeting. In between those meetings, the coach should be in touch with the planter at least monthly. In our modern age of mass communication, this all does not have to be done in person, but through e-mail, fax, and telecommunication.

The third structure suggested by Logan is that of the parent church network. This network guides pastors through the process of cultivating congregational commitment and implementing an effective strategy that results in the launching of a new congregation. In other words, this structure helps an existing church to reproduce. To form this network in a conference, two or three churches that plan on starting new congregations unite. They are planting three separate churches at the same time, but band together to deal with the common problems involved in churches that sponsor a new church plant. It serves to help churches make a commitment to church planting rather than just to hope that someday they will plant a church.

In this structure, the coach works with each of these expectant parents, guiding them through the nucleus-building phase to the birth of the new baby. Following this phase, the new church will join the New Church Incubator network, and the coach will stay with the parent church network to help them through the problems that develop after the baby is born.

A fourth structure, which Logan refers to as Leadership

Farm Systems, is also needed: a way to mobilize and raise up new leaders from the harvest who will become the future church planters. Where can such leaders be found? Throughout the system. Coaches can watch for leaders, who are found in all new church plants. These are primary candidates to be new church planters. The seminary and other educational institutions can play a major role in challenging young leaders to become church planters. It is not, however, simply changing the present number of seminarians into church planters; it is necessary to send a whole new kind of leader to the seminary, one who has been discovered in the field to have the leadership capabilities demanded for new churches. Coaches will be the primary recommenders of leaders for new churches. The assessment process will also help identify those to whom God has given the role of church planter.

This can all be accomplished with the addition of only one initial salary at the union level. This placement of coaches who can accomplish each of the four networks mentioned above is the second most strategic need. It follows the educational process for the reproducible system within Adventism in North America. The choice of personnel who will serve as coaches is vital. Only those who clearly understand the reproducible system should be so employed; otherwise, not much will happen.

With the right person as coach in a conference, with the establishment of each of the networks in the conference, and with money freed up to employ more church planters, it is conceivable that a conference could double the number of churches in the conference every three to five years. And each of these new churches would be raised out of the harvest, thus creating tremendous growth for North American Adventism.

If church planting and a reproducible system is a priority for the Adventist church in North America, then the addition of one salary to accomplish that should not be an obstacle. Church planting money must not be used for another layer of administration, but be used specifically for church planters. We must invest this minimum resource to coach the church planter if we are serious about recreating a church planting movement.

Currently, the biggest obstacle to church planting is not the finances, but finding the right people to serve as coaches. There are not many people who understand how to accomplish the reproducible system. We must find them. They are the ones who are the reproducers. No one who is not already a reproducer should be asked to be a coach. These reproducers can quickly be educated as church planting coaches. There are plenty of resources available to accomplish this training.[7]

Good coaches are resource people who ask a lot of questions and refuse to give a lot of answers. Instead, they help the church or the church planter successfully arrive at the solutions which are correct for them. Good coaching will also hold the planter and church accountable, provide positive reinforcement, and clearly see the potential in the people being coached. Logan lists a step-by-step process for coaches:

1. Listen carefully

2. Care personally

3. Affirm progress

4. Focus plans

5. Train in ministry skills

6. Challenge specifically

Summary

Creating a reproducing system begins with the educational process, educating both laity and clergy. They must develop a mission mindset and learn how to create a reproducible system for the sake of reaching the harvest of Christ. Once this education has taken place, coaches should be hired at the union level and ultimately at the conference level. These coaches will work on developing the four networks: the New

Church Incubator, the New Church Network, the Parent Church Network, and the Leadership Farm System.

Once this basic structure is in place, church planting will begin to multiply throughout Adventism. However, more is involved here than simply structure, for underlying all that has been mentioned here is the power of the Holy Spirit, poured out upon a church that is serious enough about the harvest to change its structure and thus facilitate the gathering of earth's final harvest. Let's begin now!

Notes:

1. The author wishes to acknowledge the influence of Dr. Robert E. Logan for inspiring him to consider many of the ideas suggested in this chapter.

2. Schwarz, *Natural Church Development,* 62, 63; 68, 69.

3. Ibid., 68.

4. Genesis 1:28.

5. These suggestions by Logan were made in a class on church planting at Fuller Seminary.

6. These structural suggestions were made in the same class as mentioned above.

7. One of the best coaching resources is Steve Ogne and Thomas Nebel's *Empowering Leaders Through Coaching: A Self-Study Resource Kit for Those Who Mentor Volunteer Leaders, Pastors, and Church Planters* (Church Smart Resources). For the latest church planting resources, contact NADEI at (616) 471-9220. Or view resources on the NADEI website: *www.nadei.org.*

17

Epilogue

The passion of God for the lost is what started us on this journey. The passion of Jesus for reaping the harvest must help us conclude our journey. Church planting is not just another fad that will pass, for it is rooted and grounded in the passion of God. Adventists have always believed that the work of God will finish in a blaze of soul-winning glory. Yet it is impossible for such glory to occur without serious church planting. Thus, church planting is at the heart of God's plan for reaping the final harvest. To be disobedient here is to be guilty of abandoning our duty.

We have seen that Adventism began as a church-planting movement. It has continued to be such in most of the world. It is primarily in the western world that the church abandoned the church-planting role of the pastor and substituted the shepherd/caretaking role that has dominated the Adventist ministry for most of the twentieth century. The time has come for the Adventist Church in North America to return to its roots, with its pastors firmly placed once again in the role of church planter/evangelist. The hour is too late to postpone this movement.

This book has not been simply a call to plant churches. It has been a clarion voice, calling the church to become once again a church-planting movement. That is why it is so critical, as discussed in the previous chapter, for the church to begin moving in this new direction. We must plant churches that will in turn plant churches. The harvest of God is very large and His laborers are very few, but His power is so mighty that we cannot fail.

In view of the harvest, and in response to the passion of God for the lost, it is time to make church planting the top priority of North American Adventism. It must be at the top of the agenda for the North American Division, for every union conference, for every local conference, and for every local church. The need for church planting must pulsate with every breath we take. The cry of the harvest calls the church forth to the completion of the task outlined by her Lord. Excuses must be abandoned as we view the lostness of humanity, especially in our great cities. It is no longer safe to "play" church, or we will be guilty of fiddling while Rome burns. We must move out of the safety of our cushioned pews and into the perilous streets of our communities, seeking the lost and bringing them to Jesus.

May God help us to plant these churches before it is too late. May the multiplication of churches become our all-consuming passion, until God's yearning for the lost once again flows through our veins. It's time to reap the harvest *now*. Go! Plant a church!